# St John's Beaumont

A Pictorial Celebration

Azure, an Horseshoe between in chief a Cross formy fitchy and
in base two like Crosses bendwise and one bendwise sinister Or.
For the crest, on a wreath of the colours a Wing Contournée Sable
transfixed by an Arrow bendwise sinister barb upwards Or.

# St John's Beaumont

A Pictorial Celebration

## Andrew Plant

Photography by Dominic James

SJB

First published by St John's Beaumont, 2015

ISBN 978 0 9934520 0 0

Designed by Richard & Sam Adams, Adams Associates.

Printed and bound in the UK by Northend Creative Print Solutions, Sheffield, South Yorkshire.

www.darnton.net

**Photographic credits**
Photographs by Dominic James: viii, 14, 16, 17, 18, 19, 20, 21, 27, 28, 29 (water stoup), 33, 45 (uniform, cap, badge), 60 (shrine, plaque), 61, 62, 63, 74, 75 (medals), 76, 77, 88, 89, 105 (portrait), 106, 107, 109 (medal), 110, 111, 118, 119, front cover.

Photographs by Andrew Plant: 23 (chasuble), 24, 45 (Joe Bowman), 108 (Jack Spink, string quartet), 109 (soloists, choristers).

Photographs by Nigel Luckhurst: 120, inside dust jacket flap.

All other images courtesy of St John's Beaumont, and the Archivum Britannicum Societatis Iesu.

To the boys of St John's: past, present and future

# Contents

Foreword      viii

1. The Foundation      10

2. First Admissions      34

3. World War I      56

4. Respite and Consolidation      64

5. Scouts and activities      70

6. World War II      78

7. New Elizabethans      90

Appendix      112

Acknowledgments      117

About the author      120

# Foreword

This is not an exhaustive history of St John's. To produce such a study would require far more space, and an enormous amount of additional source work, not to mention considerable financial outlay. Moreover, its overall appeal would necessarily be limited. For those interested in further investigations, Fr Hoy's little volume, printed privately for the school's centenary, remains a touchstone and a springboard; and while it does not pretend to be anything other than a personal and domestic memoir, it is written with understanding and much love for the Foundation he served for so long, particularly in its documentation of dedicated staff.

While the present anthology does, of course, include much historical material, it is primarily an exploration of the highlights that may be found in the Jesuit archives in Mayfair, and at St John's. The former is an extremely extensive and well-documented collection, while the School's holdings are, as might be expected, rather less ordered: as with many records that have passed through assorted ownership, a very large proportion of artefacts have been assembled largely by chance and personal interest, and are neither dated nor annotated. Tracing, estimating, and sifting the years through such items is always a fascinating task; and as buildings appear and disappear, eminent visitors make their entrances, and the cars get quainter or more desirable (depending on one's point of view), a portrait emerges of a unique and distinguished institution, firm in its beliefs, and confident in its idiosyncratic traditions and daily round.

In 1951, the English composer Gerald Finzi wrote, 'To shake hands with a good friend over the centuries is a pleasant thing'. The history of a school is measured in much shorter generations: those of the boys who pass unchanging through the years. Brief moments of their childhoods are chronicled here, yet their widely differing outlooks, expectations, fears, hopes, loves, enthusiasms, and ambitions remain constant. To them, and to their diverse lives and achievements, this book is dedicated.

*Andrew Plant*
Autumn 2015

*Opposite: St John's Beaumont* by Ian McKillop. Oil on canvas, 2013.

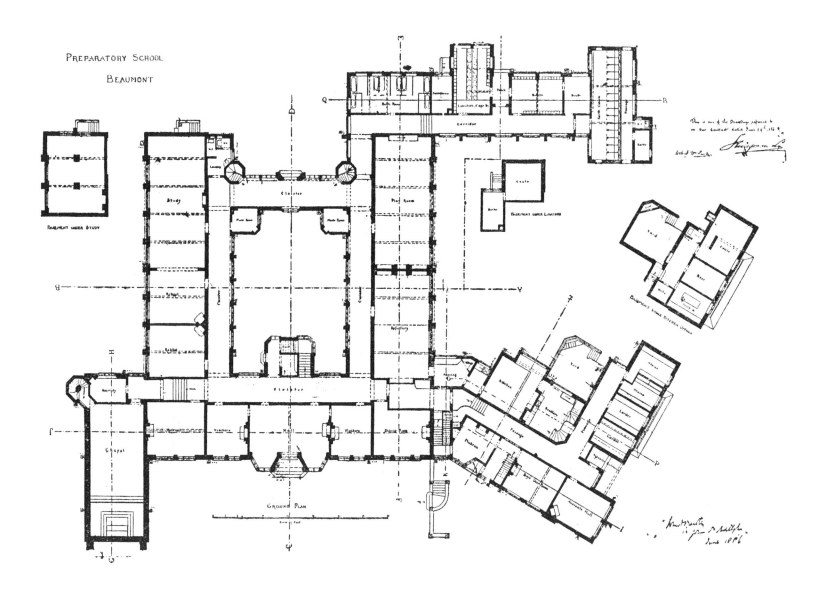

PREPARATORY SCHOOL
BEAUMONT

GROUND PLAN

# 1. The Foundation

Beaumont College was founded in 1861, and was established to provide a school of the higher class under the training of Fathers of the Society of Jesus, where that training might be united with the advantages of a mild climate and exceptionally good position within easy reach of London. A full school course of seven years prepares boys either for further university studies or for professional careers. The new junior school was opened last September. It accommodates sixty boys and is intended to give to younger and more delicate boys a thorough and suitable grounding and preparation for the college course, together with the more minute care and attention their age requires. It stands on an eminence at some distance from the college buildings, and forms a complete establishment in itself. In its construction no expense has been spared to secure the health and comfort of younger boys, and the aim of the authorities has been to make the school as much of a home as is compatible with the conditions of school life.[1]

Before the foundation of St John's, a preparatory division had been accommodated at the college, but this arrangement was not altogether satisfactory. Folk-legend traces the new school to an unfortunate accident in 1883, when a preparatory boy at Beaumont slid down a banister rail, plummeted twenty feet onto a stone floor, and was unconscious for thirty-six hours; and while this attribution may or may not be apocryphal, it has been noted that, whether by accident or design, there is hardly a single banister rail in the original buildings of St John's that a boy might use in a similar fashion. If dangerous exuberance were to be discouraged, it may be considered ironically appropriate that such an establishment should be founded very close to where, in 1852, the last recorded duel in English history had been fought. A former naval captain named Cournet and a civil engineer named Bartlemey (both French) played out their chivalric destinies in part of the Beaumont Estate off Priest Hill, opposite the farm and close to Englefield Green, which at that time was heathland and pasture. Cournet eventually died at the Barley Mow, where a knife belonging to him was apparently kept for many years. Occasionally, so the stories run,

John Francis Bentley 1839–1902. Photograph by Osmond Bentley.

*Opposite:* Bentley's final plan of St John's.

1 *The Architect*, 22 March 1889, 172

> Thurs. [Celebration of Silver Jubilee of Beaumont]
>
> 7 Boys rise. Mass followed by Te Deum. Ben. Ad Ub. Com. during Mass. Rector made short address to boys at beginning of Mass. Breakfast at 8-30. Boys had hot meat & hot rolls
>
> 10-30 Football match boys v Beaumont Union – no goals taken
>
> 1 Boys dinner – Chickens, raised pies, beef, mutton & same sweets & dessert as Community. Over about 2-5. Tables were then arranged for Community dinner in T shape.
>
> 2-30 Laying Foundation stone of new Junior School. Stone blessed – no copes or procession. Humphry de Trafford laid the stone (silver trowel) & made capital speech, appealing for funds. Fr Provincial also made speech to same effect.
>
> 3-30 Dinner in boys refectory. Menu. Oxtail. jugged hare. Chickens, Ham, R. Ducks. Beef. Saddle. Pheasants. Maraschino jelly, Orange jelly. Compote of pears. Apple Meringue Tartlets &c Grapes, bananas. pears &c &c Vido made the cakes for Community & boys. Mr Bros Boshell made a capital speech in reply to Fr Rector's toast of "Beaumont past present & to come." Dinner over 5-30.
>
> 6-30 Entertainment by Alfred Capper, thought reading, sketches. Menton &c. Stage decorated with flags & flowers: about 60 chairs from Refectory carried in, taken back by boys

the ghostly sounds of the men carrying his coffin could be heard in the pub.[2]

Since his appointment in 1884, Fr Frederick O'Hare, Rector of Beaumont, had planned the expansion of the College, the initial proposal being to rebuild it entirely at the then colossal expense of £150,000, roughly equivalent to £12m today. Following a meeting with the architect John Francis Bentley, who had already contributed enormously to the fabric of the College, and would soon receive even greater fame with his designs for Westminster Cathedral (begun in 1895), it was decided to found a separate preparatory school. The chosen location was Sanatorium Hill, although

2 Kiernan, V. G. *The Duel in European history: Honour and the Reign of Aristocracy.* Oxford: OUP (1988), 218

there was some dissent over this decision, certain advisors believing that a site closer to the parent body would be cheaper because no separate chapel would then be required. A curious cartographical quirk placed St John's in a different county and diocese to its elder, since the grounds include the ancient ditch that is the boundary between Berkshire and Surrey. At the time of the College's foundation, the whole of the Beaumont Estate was in the diocese of Southwark; however, when this diocese became too large for one bishop to serve, the new see of Portsmouth was created in 1882 by Pope Leo XIII, although this district was still under the province of Southwark.

St John Berchmans. Devotional card, Milan, 1935.

In March 1884, Bentley came to view the site and receive suggestions. One, which happily he rejected, proposed a building in 'Queen Anne style faced with timber and cement.' By March 1886, Bentley's working drawings had been prepared and the estimated cost was £15,000. In the event the lowest tender was for £18,553 plus £250 for excavations and £90 for the construction of a drive from Priest Hill. The Clerk of Works was to receive four guineas a week or three guineas with board and lodging.[3]

Bentley's plans and drawings for St John's date from May 1884 to August 1893, and are held in the Victoria and Albert Museum on permanent loan. There are some 260 sheets of designs, elevations, sections and details. Some of his most attractive and beautiful work, particularly that for stained glass, is extremely fragile, and, at the time of writing, cannot be unrolled or photographed. Many are signed and inscribed with Bentley's address (13 John Street, Adelphi) and annotated by him, or the draughtsman. Winefride de L'Hôpital, the architect's daughter, wrote a comprehensive biography of her father that remains an invaluable source for the history of St John's. Her accounts of the furnishings and decorations are especially intriguing, as much has been altered in the intervening years.

It will be observed that the ground floor rooms of the central portion are designed for the reception and entertainment of guests; the doors on either side of the elegant entrance hall open respectively into drawing and dining rooms, both with wainscoted dados and fine details to ornament chimney-pieces, doors, and windows ... The charming bow-windowed turret rooms above the hall are used as sitting-rooms for priests and masters.[4] In the east and west wings are contained the school buildings proper ... spacious, light and airy chambers with details as attractive and harmonious as in the reception rooms, though necessarily characterised by greater simplicity. In the play-room ... the wainscoted deep blue dado, the broad and rather low arched recesses on either side of the fireplace, the high moulded chimney-piece of beautiful form,

3 Hoy, David. *The Story of St John's Beaumont.* [Old Windsor]: St John's Beaumont (1987), 2. At a conservative estimate, the total equivalent in today's money would be around £2m.

4 Now the Headmaster's study, and the school office.

Three of St John's oaks.

with its blue and white painted tiles ... One can scarcely conceive a pleasanter apartment for children to play in, when they cannot be out of doors.[5]

5 L'Hôpital, Winefride. *Westminster Cathedral and its architect: the making of the architect.* London: Hutchinson & Co. (1919), Vol. II, 512

6 Both were renamed at the School centenary (1988) after two martyrs. Chapel, the junior dormitory, became Morse after Fr Henry Morse, who died in 1645 following a ministry to the sick during the Great Plague of London. Infirmary became Southwell, after the poet Robert Southwell, executed at Tyburn in 1595.

7 Beaumont College possessed similar symbols, such as a Corpus Christi oak: see *The Beaumont Review*, no. XCIV (July 1918), 403. NB: The numbering of the College's magazine varied during its run, so the relevant bibliographical references in this volume may also appear inconsistent.

The Playroom to which L'Hôpital refers was originally the Common Room. On the first floor, what is now Rudiments A (until recently the Marking Room) was originally the ward of the Sick Bay. Matron was accommodated in what is now Rudiments B; until summer 2014, it was the classroom for Great Figures B. The tiny areas at the top of the stairs leading to Chapel Dormitory and Infirmary Dormitory[6] were Brushing Rooms; the modern WCs opposite them were originally closets for the housemaids.

The foundation stone was laid by Sir Humphrey de Trafford on 21st October 1886, the Silver Jubilee of Beaumont College being marked at the same time. The site was further prepared in 1887 by the planting of three oak trees, the symbolism of which allied the new establishment with Church and State.[7] The first of these, planted on 29th April, close to what is now the small pond to the south of the façade, marked the Golden Jubilee of Queen Victoria, which had been celebrated nationally a few days before. The remaining two trees were both planted on 1st December 1887. The English Martyrs oak, close to the new chapel, commemorated those fifty-four worthies who had been beatified the previous year (a further nine would follow in 1895), of whom eight would also feature in the stained glass of the new entrance hall. All had refused to acknowledge royal supremacy over the Pope. The curiously-worded plaque marking the third tree, planted a little further down the drive — 'His Holiness/Pope Leo the 13th/Jubilee Oak' — is in honour of the Pope in office at the time of Victoria's Jubilee, who was that month celebrating the Golden Jubilee of his ordination.[8] A fourth oak was added in 2002 to mark the Golden Jubilee of H.M. Queen Elizabeth II.

The layout of the entire site is almost exactly as originally intended, the principal difference between Bentley's first and second plans being the positioning of the chapel. It is clear that lack of space determined its eventual construction to the left of the main elevation, rather than to the right as was first envisaged. With the exception of the Gothic chapel, the predominant influence is French Renaissance, as Pevsner[9] terms the building, including the elegant little terrace overlooking the grounds. Bentley's influence was felt throughout the building, from the gorgeous palace-like exterior to the humblest grating, cupboard door, fire-screen or towel rail. Panelling, skirting boards, window frames, wash-stands, refectory tables, mirrors, floor joists, shelves, wardrobes, balustrades, grates, fenders, and even the coal chute were all his concern. His brief was to build for sixty boys, and this was carried out almost to the letter, with sixty-one seats for pupils in chapel and two dormitories housing thirty each. While it is easily outflanked by other establishments in date of foundation, St John's may claim to be the oldest purpose-built preparatory school in the country.

Simplicity of design, high curved ceilings and great windows, give an impression of grandeur and lightness which please the eye as it surveys the wide and lofty dormitories, and the proportions of the cool, spacious galleries, which surround a cloister garden are no less attractive. Yet one has only to study the kitchen with its high windows and ceiling giving plenty of light and air; the beautifully proportioned infirmary, farthest from the noise of the school, yet so placed that it can be cheerful with sunshine all day; the wash-place with its fine array of windows; and one can see that beauty and practicality go hand-in-hand.[10]

It may be imagined with what excitement the youngsters of the 'Preparatory Side' watched the great palace rising on the Surrey hill-side and speculated upon their chances of being admitted among the first inhabitants. Our favourite walk in those days was among foundations and inchoate walls and miniature railways ...[11]

8 The Vatican holds a brief film from 1896 by La Cineteca Italiana of Pope Leo XIII, which remains the oldest footage of a Pope known to exist (and who is therefore possibly the oldest person known to be filmed). The skullcap in which he was crowned Pope was given by Leo XIII himself to Francis O'Gorman, and is now held by St John's.

9 Pevsner, Nikolaus. *The Buildings of England: Berkshire.* Middlesex: Penguin Books Ltd.(1966), 190

10 *Beaumont Centenary Celebrations 1861–1961. Centenary Programme.* Old Windsor: Beaumont College (n.d.).

11 C.L. [almost certainly Cuthbert Lattey, the first Head Boy], 'The First Year at St John's' in *The Beaumont Review*, no. LXXVI (July 1913), 88

St John's, 2015.

*Opposite, clockwise from top:*
St Stanislaus Kostka; Keystone;
St Aloysius; Kostka's device;
Green rams.

The magnificent main entrance is richly theatrical, barely short of a stage set, the honey-coloured stone and red tiled roofs contrasting most pleasingly with the flamboyant bands of polychromatic red brick and Monk Park stone that would later characterize Bentley's designs for Westminster Cathedral.[12] On the keystone of the main arch is the IHS badge of the Society of Jesus, while the pilasters bear medallions containing reliefs of SS Stanislaus Kostka (who also appears in the east window of the chapel) and Aloysius, the patron of youth, with their initials. The porch is surmounted by two balconies flanked by polygonal towers, between which two *putti* bear the motto and symbols of Kostka. Above this panel is a dormer window flourishing an almost excessively ornate pelmet, and finally a white triple-tiered lantern somewhat reminiscent of a lighthouse, its ogee cap crowned with an elaborate finial. It must be said that this feature is better appreciated from the rear of the building, which is more Georgian. Here the pelmet does not intrude and a clock has been thoughtfully and tastefully placed to be of best use. The curious 'green rams' on the inner pilasters of the porch are rare bestial versions of the more familiar foliate head, and may appear slightly sinister to twenty-first century eyes. In general, the majority of 'green animals' to be found anywhere are cats or lions; but here the image is undoubtedly purely a decorative feature, its fascinating but confusing iconography still not fully understood. Many of Bentley's contemporaries, such as George Gilbert Scott Jnr, also incorporated such grotesques into Victorian buildings, thereby foreshadowing new traditions and meanings acquired by the image in the next century, notably in the work of John Piper.

The Chapel features Perpendicular windows and also bears a small turret, again ogee-crowned, on the side away from the main façade over the stairs to the tribune (organ loft). The former Infirmary to the right of the main façade features a thin oriel window crowned with a half-ogee cap. A charming touch of domesticity results from the carved panel on the chimney-stack, showing the selfless companion of St Roch (or Rocco), patron of the sick (*d* 1327), complete with loaf of bread: legend says that the saint was saved by food brought by a starving dog. Other exterior

12 St John's has two larger neighbours and contemporaries in historical, geographical and architectural terms, both designed by William Henry Crossland. The spectacular Holloway Sanatorium (now Virginia Park) opened in 1885, and the similarly ornate Royal Holloway College was founded the following year. Both illustrate the then prevailing fashion for contrasting brick and stone (inspired, in the case of the College, by Château de Chambord in the Loire Valley).

*Left:* St Roch's companion.

*Right:* SJB cypher.

*Opposite:* Grotesques under windows of dormitories.

13 *The History of St. Stanislaus' College Beaumont: a record of fifty years 1861–1911.* Old Windsor: The Beaumont Review Office [Beaumont College] (1911), 150

14 It is not impossible that the tiger skin had some connection with the dramatic exploits of Sidney Meyer (Elements II in 1906), who was born in India, where he lived until nine years old. In 1902, there being no 'health and safety' regulations to contest, he had persuaded his father to take him on his first tiger hunt, joining a party of native beaters, and eleven hunters on elephants. When the furious wounded quarry attacked the elephant he was riding, Meyer remarked sanguinely, 'I remember distinctly wishing I had stayed at home'; but, the tiger having been dispatched, he assured his readers it had been a 'most eventful day'. See *The Beaumont Review*, no. XLVII (June 1906), 406

15 L'Hôpital, ibid, 512. Much of the glass is hand-painted, notably the decorative initials in the lights under each portrait.

embellishments are placed at the rear elevation, notably around the huge windows of the two dormitories. These smaller carvings, including further felines, are more exposed to the elements and therefore less well-preserved; at least one now bears a terrifying resemblance to Tolkien's Witch-king, as portrayed in Peter Jackson's films.

'Inside the hall there are the bold chimney-piece, the doors with their curious entablatures, the marble mosaic floor, the stained glass of the oriel windows — everywhere the enduring expression of high and delicate thought.'[13] At the time of writing, a fitted carpet hides the mosaic, but its richness, and welcoming SALVE, may be seen in old photographs. A few years after the school's opening, a concatenation of heavy furniture, potted plants, and a formidable tiger skin had transformed the entrance hall into a colonial outpost of the British Raj: the reigning monarch was, after all, Empress of India.[14]

The woodwork throughout the house is painted, generally in Bentley's favourite tone of dark greenish-blue; the plaster work above being as a rule white. The paint chosen for the hall is another of his favourite tints, well known to those familiar with his colour schemes, namely a mellow Venetian red. The stained glass in the upper lights of the great bow windows of the entrance displays, within enwreathed medallions, heads of the most prominent among the many staunch Englishmen who suffered death for their faith and principles in the sixteenth and seventeenth centuries. The arabesque design, executed mainly in grisaille, and the ornamental leading of the quarries in the lower lights are both extremely graceful.[15]

Photocards, undated.

ENTRANCE HALL,
ST. JOHN'S, BEAUMONT.

In contrast to the opulent entrance hall, early images of the main galleries disclose decidedly plain interiors, the monastic overtones highly apparent. Indeed, for some years the rear lodge of St John's housed the first convent in England of the Little Servants of the Mother of God, founded by Mother Taylor.

The dedication of the new school was not decided until March 1888. At that point, the Fathers alighted on the name of St John Berchmans, a young Jesuit saint who had been canonised that year, along with Peter Claver and Alphonsus Rodriguez. This delay explains why the building bears no markings to identify it precisely, except the small cyphers 'SJB' by the rear doors, and related carvings by the east window of the chapel. These are, no doubt, some of Bentley's last exterior designs. When the chivalrous boy-saint Stanislaus Kostka was chosen as the Patron of Beaumont, his coat of arms and crest were assumed by the College, although the design underwent a number of seemingly unofficial stages, only emerging in its familiar form around 1885.[16] The College was not, in fact, entitled to any arms until the College of Heralds regularized their use of Kostka's in 1962, with assistance (presumably of a financial nature) from Major G. T. M. Scrope.[17] The motto was adopted later, and is taken from the liturgical office of the saint. As the Junior School, St John's used the Arms by default, and continues to do so.

Front gallery. Photocard, undated.

*Below left:* Kostka's arms described in Latin.

*Below:* St John's crest on a chasuble, as used in chapel.

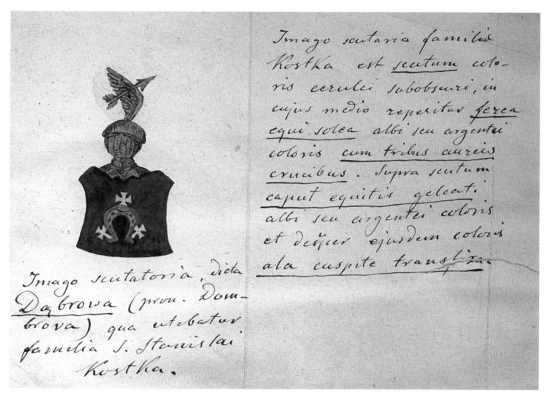

16 Sexton, Fr George. 'The Beaumont Crest', *The Beaumont Review*, vol. XVII, no. 142 (December 1934), 472. Sexton was Headmaster of St John's from 1918 to 1929.

17 *The Beaumont Review*, vol. XXXI, no. 205 (March 1963), 297. The family had several sons who were named Geoffrey after the fourteenth-century Chief Justice, including the Head Boy of St John's for the academic year 1932–33.

*Left:* Lantern and clock.

*Right:* Chapel turret.

In 1888, Queen Victoria had just begun her fifty-first year on the throne, with Robert Cecil as Prime Minister. That year, as Hoy remarked, the Miners' Federation of Great Britain, the Scottish Labour Party and the London General Omnibus Company were founded, Karl Benz invented his 1½ horse-power petrol-driven automobile, and so marked the birth of the car industry; while, for the more impoverished, Parliament passed an Act permitting bicycles on the road (the pneumatic tyre also being patented in this year), providing a bell was fitted. In April, the Concertgebouw opened in Amsterdam, followed a few months later by London's Lyric Theatre in Shaftesbury Avenue. The Whitechapel murders began, the Woodbine cigarette was first marketed,

CHAPEL, ST. JOHN'S, BEAUMONT.

Photocard, undated.

and Gilbert and Sullivan's eleventh operetta *The Yeomen of the Guard* received its premiere at the Savoy Theatre. Irving Berlin, Lawrence of Arabia, and T. S. Eliot were born, while Henry James, Rider Haggard and Thomas Hardy were at the height of their powers. Van Gogh began his iconic series of the Arles *Sunflowers,* and Oscar Wilde's *The Happy Prince* was published — as was W. E. Henley's triumphant poem *Invictus,* which, in more recent years, has become a cherished, not to say ubiquitous, feature of the annual verse-speaking competition at St John's.

Life had been progressing for some weeks before the first term was interrupted for the official opening. At Beaumont College, there was a Solemn High Mass with a sermon by Fr Bernard Vaughan, perhaps the most famous preacher of his day. He took as his text, 'Whatever thy hand is able to do, do it earnestly', and delivered a homily on St John Berchman as a practical model for his young followers: ' ... the one secret of whose sanctity and greatness was that as the various duties of a life came

The new arrival announced in *The Times*, September 26, 1888.

*Opposite left:* Jesuit foundation.

*Opposite right: Ecce Homo* and *Coronation with Thorns.*

before him, he gave to each, for the love of God, his whole soul and strength.'[18] Following this, one hundred and eight guests sat down to luncheon in the College refectory, although the Minister's rapture was evidently somewhat modified: in a rueful comparison to the College's patronal Silver Jubilee, his journal entry noted laconically, 'Like St Stanislaus (without the cake)'. In the afternoon Dr Butt blessed and declared the new preparatory school open. The tiny choir of new boys was augmented by members from the College, the first treble being Francis de Zulueta (later a Fellow of All Souls', Oxford, and Regius Professor of Civil Law, the first such Catholic since the Reformation to hold such a post). Years later, Winefride de L'Hôpital recalled attending the ceremony as a child, being especially impressed by the electric lighting. The school had its own generators at the time, although some parts were lit by gas, and a former pupil recalled that it was a recognized practice to go to the generating room to have one's penknife electrified.[19] Even by 1906 the science was still considered sufficiently novel for a laudatory article to appear that year in *The Beaumont Review* explaining the workings of three types of lamp, and providing elucidations of such exotic terminology as 'volts', 'amperes' and 'watts'.[20]

The chapel was not completed until some twenty-five years after the school was first opened, and an early photograph emphasizes its rural surroundings. Naturally, almost everything within it was also Bentley's work, although not all the furnishings now in place were present at the opening. The silver sanctuary lamp, also Bentley's creation, was presented in 1889 by the Old Boys of the Beaumont Union. In 1896, the first wooden altar was replaced by the current example in grey Derbyshire marble, the gift of Fr Ignatius O'Gorman (Headmaster 1902–1904), Paul Cullen, and George Rendel, a former Civil Lord of the Admiralty, who donated £200 for the altar before his conversion to Catholicism.

18 *The Weekly Register.* London (September 29, 1888).

19 *The Beaumont Review*, no. LXXVI (July 1913), 89

20 *The Beaumont Review*, no. XLVI (March 1906), 335

21 Ibid., 514

Its frontal, very original in design, is constructed with a five-fold arcading, whose outward curving shafting produces a fan-like effect. The panels are filled with slightly concave slabs of cipollino, a clear pale green marble of excellent figure. The painted reredos is in the form of a triptych in a gilt frame very richly carved and burnished, whose central subject is the Crucifixion.[21]

*Above:* Bench end.

*Below:* Tabernacle.

22 L'Hôpital, ibid., 513

23 Ibid., 551

24 Ibid., 565

25 Like Bentley, Voysey was noted not only for designing buildings, but all fixtures and fittings therein.

26 *The Beaumont Review*, no. XXXVII (October 1903), 209

[Photographs convey] the quiet charm of this lovely chapel. To the tone of the fumed oak, which is warm and not too light, contrast has been obtained by painting the west gallery, also constructed in oak, a deep blue, a procedure which has aroused adverse comment, though personally we think Bentley's bold expedient of employing colour across this end is amply justified by the result.[22]

[The chapel contains] three stained glass windows designed by the architect, the gift of Mrs W. Dalglish-Bellasis. The five-light east window of the chancel is a noble and harmonious production, in whose central and tallest light is seen our Lord robed and enthroned in majesty; above, angels uphold flowing garlands and drapery behind Him, while beneath His feet stands St Michael in knightly equipment. Our Lady and St Joseph in suppliant attitudes appear in the adjoining light on the left, while on the right are St John the Baptist and St Peter, similarly represented. The outer lights are occupied with four saints of the Order of Jesus, St Ignatius and St Stanislaus (left), St Francis Xavier and St John Berchmans (right). The topmost space in each division of the window is filled with angels and the tracery is treated with light and elegant grisaille work. In the side windows of the sanctuary are depicted four events in Our Lord's Passion: the Agony and the Kiss of Judas on the Epistle side; the Ecce Homo and the Coronation of Our Lord with Thorns on the Gospel side.[23]

The elaborately twisted electric fittings attained, in the (admittedly biased) opinion of L'Hôpital, 'the acme of simplicity and grace possible in wrought ironwork.'[24] Aside from the gallery and the *sedilia* in the sanctuary, seating comprised four stalls at the West end (facing East) for the staff, the remainder, facing inwards across the nave, allocated to the pupils: thirty on the north side, thirty-one on the south. The extra seat may simply have been Bentley allowing himself some leeway, but it was assigned at some point to the housemaster, while three of the other places were also commandeered for staff as the community grew. On the bench-ends, set as precisely as chessmen, are carved heads of priests (each sporting a zucchetto, or pileolus), boys, and — on the headmaster's stalls — one devotional female. Bentley just missed seeing the installation of his impressive tabernacle, studded with a garnet and adorned prolifically with lapis lazuli and mother-of-pearl, which arrived on 6 October 1902. Its ornate craftsmanship, including the Gothic inscription *Cor Jesu charitatis victima miserere nobis*, was the work of the highly reputable firm Thomas Elsley & Co., of Great Titchfield Street, for whom the architect C. F. Voysey (1857–1941) would design a quantity of items.[25] By 1903, it was reported that the reredos was the only thing not finished, but this confidence was somewhat premature.[26] The oak panelling around the sanctuary,

including the canopied niches, was installed in 1909, having been completed by Bentley's son after his father's death. Two other canopies, along with four wooden statues of the Sacred Heart, Our Lady, St Joseph and St John Berchmans, were obtained from Bruges in 1910. The Stations of the Cross were put in place by Fr Green.[27] In future years, Bentley's work would even be celebrated on the label for school prizes, a succession of typical arches framing a dutiful pupil, kneeling at his master's feet.

An undated prospectus for the Beaumont Foundation recommended St John's as a suitable establishment 'where young and delicate boys may receive more care and individual attention.' The general tone and directions of this fascinating document evoke a wholly-vanished world such as described by Thomas Hughes, not least in the expectation that once boys reached College age they were encouraged to 'manage their own games and amusements and to maintain order and discipline among themselves without undue interference from Masters.' At St John's, notwithstanding a softer reassurance that 'the youngest boys are taught by a resident Governess', a firm party line was drawn from the outset. Expectations of progress were high, considerable weight being placed on attaining standards suitable for navy entrance, the course to be continued at a suitable college. Before the end of the first term, St John's had fifty-eight pupils in its charge, delicate and otherwise.

*Above:* Decoration on water stoup.

*Below:* Prize label.

27 Headmaster, 1908–17.

Pages from an early prospectus.

*The Junior School*

20. Before the removal of a boy three months' notice is required, or three months' pension must be paid.

21. The Authorities reserve to themselves the liberty of resigning at once the charge of any boy for whose correction the ordinary means are found ineffectual, or who is deriving no benefit from his stay.

22. The times during which Parents may visit their boys are from 1.30 to 5.30 p.m. on Sundays, Tuesdays, and Thursdays. Boys may not receive visits during Study hours.

23. *Exeats* are not allowed unless with special permission and for grave reasons.

24. **THE JUNIOR SCHOOL.** (1) The Junior School, St. John's—is a Preparatory School for the College, and provides a separate establishment, where young and delicate boys may receive more care and individual attention. Both College and Junior School are under the same management, and the general regulations are the same in both.

(2) The number of boys at St. John's is limited to 60, and the age ranges from 8 to 13.

(3) The two highest Forms at St. John's correspond to the two lowest at the College and the work is arranged to suit the new Navy requirements. There are, in addition, lower divisions intended for boys whose home education has not reached the standard of either of these Forms, but no boy will be received who cannot read and write fairly. The youngest boys are taught by a resident Governess.

(4) A resident Matron pays particular attention to all that concerns the health, comfort, cleanliness and tidiness of the boys.

N.B.—**A SCHOLARSHIP** of 30 guineas a year, tenable for two years, and continued under certain conditions for two further years, is open for competition to boys under thirteen, inside and outside the College, who show themselves well fitted to enter the Lower Fourth Form. This supposes them to have begun the work of the First Form about the age of ten. It is strongly recommended that boys should be sent at such an age and so prepared, as to be able to enter the First Form about the age of ten or the Preparatory Class about the age of nine. Failures in the Army and still more in the Navy Entrance Examinations are generally due to the neglect of this precaution.

## Dietary.

7.30 a.m. (at Junior School 8 a.m.) Breakfast. Tea or coffee, bread and butter, toast, porridge and milk, meat, fish or eggs.

10.45 a.m., bread and soup.

1 p.m., Dinner. Soup occasionally, two courses of meat (or of fish on Fridays), vegetables, sweet, cheese, beer.

5 p.m., Tea.

7.30 p.m., Supper. Tea, bread and butter, toast, jam or marmalade. At Junior School, hot milk or cocoa, bread and jam or marmalade.

Extra diet at Supper, though considered unnecessary by the School Authorities, will be provided, if desired, at the cost of 6d. per meal, *i.e.*, £3 10s. per half year.

Hampers are allowed on the understanding that their contents are consumed during meals.

# Terms.

THE ORDINARY COURSE AT THE COLLEGE AND JUNIOR SCHOOL ... 90 GUINEAS PER ANN.
THE ARMY COURSE, NAVY COURSE AND SPECIAL TUITION ... 100 ,, ,,

This Pension, to be paid half-yearly in advance in September and March, includes Board, Tuition and Laundry.

The only necessary extras are the following :—

| | |
|---|---|
| USE OF BOOKS AND STATIONERY ... ... ... ... | 10/– per Annum. |
| POCKET MONEY (at 6d. per week) ... ... | £1 per Annum (for boys under 12). |
| ,, ,, (at 1/– per week) ... | £2 per Annum (for boys over 12). |
| CRICKET SUBSCRIPTION :—For Higher Forms ... ... | £1 1s. per Annum. |
| ,, ,, For Middle Forms ... ... | 15/– ,, |
| ,, ,, For Lower Forms ... ... | 10/6 ,, |
| ,, ,, For Junior School ... ... | 7/6 ,, |
| FOOTBALL SUBSCRIPTION ... ... ... ... ... | 5/– ,, |
| CADET CORPS, College ... ... ... ... | £1 per Annum. Uniform 25/– |
| PHYSICAL DRILL (Sandow system), St. John's ... ... | 10/– per Annum. |
| SUBSCRIPTION to *Beaumont Review* ... ... ... ... | 3/– ,, |

The Lawn Tennis and Rowing Clubs are optional. For those who wish to join them, the Subscription to the Rowing Club is 10/– per Term or £1 per Annum; to the Lawn Tennis Club, 2/6 per term.

The following Subjects are taught at the option of Parents. The instruction is in every case by a Lay Professor :—

| | | | |
|---|---|---|---|
| DRAWING ... ... ... per Annum £5 | FENCING ... ... per Annum £1 10. |
| MUSIC (2 lessons per week) ... per Lesson 2/6 | BOXING ... ... ,, £1 10. |
| GYMNASTICS... ... ... per Annum £1 | SWIMMING and CARPENTRY ... per Lesson, 6d. |

---

Letters or Telegrams should be addressed :—

BEAUMONT, or, ST. JOHN'S, BEAUMONT,
OLD-WINDSOR. OLD-WINDSOR.

The College is reached by Train from Paddington to Windsor, G.W.R., or from Waterloo to Windsor or Egham, S.W.R. An Omnibus at Windsor meets the chief Trains from London.

---

*N.B.—The receipt of this Prospectus by the Parent or Guardian of a boy subsequently entering the School will be treated as an agreement to abide by all its provisions. Special attention is directed to those numbered 19—23.*

*St John's Beaumont College,*
engraver unknown.

To their brand new school many of the boys would have come in a four-wheeler cab from the Great Western Railway station at Windsor. The cabman charged four shillings. It was not until 1895 that a horse-bus began to run from Windsor Castle to The Bells of Ouseley. It ran six times a day and the fare was sixpence ... The whole setting of St John's was unashamedly rural. As the young gentlemen drove from Windsor, wearing either their Sunday Eton suits perhaps with diminutive top hats, or their everyday Norfolk jackets and knee-breeches, they will have seen few houses along the route ... The riverside would have been more like a riverside should be, though as early as 1904 people were complaining that the lovely poplars had been cut back too vigorously ... The way through Runnymede was no more than a track. On St John's drive the bordering trees were in their infancy and there were no railings to prevent the cattle straying from the Beaumont Farm.[28]

28 Hoy, ibid, 4–7.

St John's Beaumont

Peter Knott 55

While many early photos of the school are undated, the images in this chapter probably give as good an idea of the first decades as any. The felled poplars referred to above are not, of course, those famously lamented by the Jesuit poet Gerard Manley Hopkins (who died in 1889 during St John's first summer term); but the school's environment was also a 'sweet especial rural scene', and much of its early splendour may still be glimpsed. The founders established their institution in lush grounds that were nonetheless open and uncluttered, the surrounding landscape 'plotted and pierced': an idyllic setting for a 'pied beauty' of brick and stone in which to praise God for dappled things.

Watercolour by Fr Peter Knott SJ, the first Catholic chaplain at Eton.

# 2. First Admissions

*Opposite:* Returning pupils, undated (*c.* late 1970s).

1 Catalogue of the English Province of the Society of Jesus. London: Burns and Oates (1888), 23. *Min.* (i.e. *Min. Dom.* or *Minister of the House*) denoted the holder as Father Superior, while still less in seniority to the Superior, who was the Rector of Beaumont College. The four academics at St John's were therefore dependent on the larger community at Beaumont. *Præf. mor* would today be known as the Deputy Headmaster in charge of discipline — hence *mor* (morals) — and pastoral care, as distinct from *Præf. stud.,* the Prefect of Studies in charge of academic matters. *Dir. Apost. Orat.* means Director of the Apostleship of Prayer (advocates of living one's life as a daily offering to God). The remainder of the abbreviations merely refer to *Doc* (i.e. teacher), the class (Figures or Elements) and the number of years each member of staff had been teaching in a Jesuit institution. The author is grateful to Fr Adrian Porter SJ for his clarification of these matters.

2 This terminology, based on the cumulative educational model of the mediæval *trivium*, is retained at St John's to this day, although others have now been added: two in the Pre-Prep Department (Blandyke and Berchmans) and one in the Middle School (Bellarmine), all preceding Lower Elements. This in turn is followed by Upper Elements, and Lower and Upper Figures. The current top two years (Figures and Rudiments) would have been the lowest at the College, where boys would then have proceeded through Grammar, Syntax, Poetry and Rhetoric.

3 *The Beaumont Lists for fifty years, 1861–1911.* Old Windsor: Beaumont College (*c.*1911).

When St John's opened in 1888, the staff as listed[1] 'In Domo Præparatoria' consisted of

P. Jonannes Lynch, *Min., Præf. mor., Catech. class. præp., Dir. Apost. Orat.*
Fridericus Akehurst, *Doc. fig., ann. 4 mag.*
Johannes O'Neil, *Doc. elem., ann. 4 mag.*
Ignatius O'Gorman, *Doc. school. præp., ann. 1 mag., Assist. præf. mor.*

All but the last named had been transferred from the preparatory department at the College, so some of the new boys would have already known them. They were the staff for whom the four seats at the west end of the chapel — now all designated simply as HEADMASTER — were designed. The highest class was Figures division II, but both establishments possessed classes named Rudiments, as well as Upper and Lower divisions of Elements and Figures.[2] This duplication sometimes obscures exactly which boys were at St John's in its earliest years, but some assistance may be gained through inspection of official records of alumni, particularly the *Beaumont Lists.*[3] Names may also be gleaned from volumes listing the sacrament of confirmation, or from membership of such bodies as the Apostleship of Prayer.

The Archivum Britannicum Societatis Iesu holds a substantial collection of portraits, among which are representatives of the first St John's boys, inhabitants of a world that has now wholly vanished. While some would achieve more widely-documented success, one may only guess at the personalities, social aspirations, ambitions and dreams of those whose entire lives are now each represented by a single formal image from their youth. In a poignant contrast to current practice, where almost every moment of waking life is recorded for posterity, these pictures would have been particularly significant to the subjects. In many cases they marked only the commencement of their senior schooling, but in others the termination of their childhood, before encroaching adult life claimed them.

The earliest image so far traced of St John's as a body is a formal photograph from 1889, presumably taken at the end of the first academic year. Names have been added in pencil but not all the boys are listed, and the left panel is damaged, so some

_et._

Davas

Silverlop ?

s. Taylor, Paul ?(Sykes)

man . H.Dickens . Ellis.

G. Gillow. Hibbert . O'Reiley

Carr. Sidgreaves. Frescoe. Goldie

Quill, F Sherin. Mathews. H. Hibbert

J. Woodlock. Oliphant. A. Stones
                        Bretherton

Lindo-Staunton

St John's, 1889.

C. Lattey
Pownall . ?
? Hendrick , Becket , Bamboo
? Boussot
(Charles) ? Lumisden . C. Sherrin Zuluetta
Hay . G. Dickens . Melhado .
Rookley . Bagshaw . Woodlock
S. Corran
Melhado . G. Scott . Vaughn
Bunbury
Murphy . Davies . Kemp . Knight
(Gui?) Adolph . Adolph

1889

St. John's, Beaumont.

*Above left:* Eduardo de Fresco. Studio portrait, 1887. St John's 1888–89.

*Above right:* Eduardo de Fresco. Studio portrait, 1889. He arrived at Beaumont College as a preparatory pupil on 6 June 1887, so would have joined St John's almost immediately. From 1886, boys were admitted to the Royal Naval College, Dartmouth between the ages of thirteen and fourteen; in 1903, its sister establishment opened at Osborne, Isle of Wight, to take them for two years, before they proceeded to Dartmouth for further training. de Fresco's nautical attire is probably one of the first indications of the destination many St John's boys would choose, following membership of the Navy class at school. By 1914, the fleet required many men, and a large number of raw recruits had their training cut short in order to enlarge the ranks. One of the first cadets from St John's, Geoffrey Harold, who had only just joined HMS *Hogue*, was a mere fifteen-year-old midshipman when he died during the sinking of the cruiser in 1914. The College at Osborne was the setting for Terence Rattigan's 1946 stage-play *The Winslow Boy* (the seminal film starring Robert Donat, and directed by Anthony Asquith, followed two years later), based on the true story of a legal battle to exonerate a pupil who was falsely accused of petty theft. The boy in question, George Archer-Shee, was killed at Ypres in October 1914, aged nineteen. He was an alumnus of Stonyhurst.

*Opposite lower left:* Wilfrid Arnold Rooke Ley. Signed studio portrait, 1889. St John's 1889; Beaumont College 1887–91 (transferred from the preparatory department to St John's). Christ Church, Oxford; became a solicitor.

*Opposite lower right:* B. Wilkinson. Signed studio portrait, May 1890.

*Clockwise from top left:* Philip Sidney Ronayne Conron. Studio portrait 1890 (12 years old). St John's 1888; Beaumont College until 1891. Entered the RN in 1892, and was a Lieutenant in 1900, serving in the gunboat *Pigeon*, and, from 1903, in the Channel Fleet aboard the armoured cruiser *Bedford*.

Robert Tidmarsh. Signed studio portrait, 1890. Beaumont College 1890–91.

Nicholas Daniel Lyons. Signed studio portrait, 15 October 1890. Beaumont College 1890–97; rowed in VIII; became engineer in Sheffield.

Francis ['Frank'] Murphy. Signed studio portrait, October 1890. Beaumont 1890–96, possibly at St John's. Trinity College, Dublin; Lieutenant Royal Field Artillery; Reserve of Officers.

*Clockwise from top left:*
Robert Hay & Alexander Hay. Signed studio double portrait, December 1890. Both attended Beaumont College 1889–97. Alexander became a Captain in 3rd Batt. East Surrey regiment and served in the Boer War (medal and three clasps).

John O'Neil-Power. Signed studio portrait, February 1891. St John's 1889; Beaumont College 1890–97. Captain, Waterford Artillery (Militia).

Bertram George Lynch-Staunton. Signed studio portrait, 28 February 1891. St John's 1888; Beaumont College 1889–94. An accomplished solo treble at St John's, he later became priest of Folkestone in the diocese of Southwark.

Edmund George Gould. Studio portrait, 3 February 1891. Possibly St John's; Beaumont College 1889–95. Lieutenant, 2nd Buffs; served in the Boer War (medal and four clasps).

*Clockwise from top left:* Gerald Thornton Salvin, of Croxdale Hall, Durham (the family home since 1402). Signed studio portrait, August 1891. St John's 1888; Beaumont College 1889–96.

Henry Gerard Oliphant, RVO, MVO, DSO. Signed ['Harry'] studio portrait, 1891. Son of General Sir J. Oliphant. St John's 1888; Beaumont College 1889–91. His distinguished naval career began in 1897 as a midshipman, travelling to China aboard the cruiser *Powerful*. He then became Second Lieutenant on HMY *Victoria and Albert*, served in the Mediterranean on the battleship *Renown*, and soon joined the flagship cruiser *Euryalus*. He rose to the rank of Commander.

Hubert Pinto-Leite. Signed studio portrait, 1891. Possibly St John's; Beaumont College 1890–98. Gonville & Caius College, Cambridge, then became a doctor.

Richard Plowden. Signed studio portrait, 1891. By 1897 he was a midshipman on the 14,900-ton battleship *Cæsar* in the Mediterranean; in 1903 he had become a Lieutenant aboard the cruiser *Psyche*, on which vessel he served in Australia for at least two years. He also rose to the rank of Commander.

annotations have been lost. However, the identities, if not the exact faces, of the majority of these boys may be ascertained with some degree of certainty, including some of the individual portraits encountered in the archives. Conron, Hay, Lynch-Staunton, Oliphant and Rooke Ley are present, as is [de] Fresco, who then passes out of current knowledge, as he did not proceed to Beaumont afterwards.[4] There is also a Murphy, who was possibly some relation to Frank, but the surname was not uncommon at Beaumont. Wilfrid Arnold Rooke Ley had joined the preparatory department of Beaumont in 1886, while Vernon John Benbow, Alban Leo Carr, George Gillow, Alfred John Kemp, Cuthbert Lattey (the first Head Boy and a future Jesuit), and Gerald Woodlock are recorded as being there from 1887; so all these boys are part of the initial intake who followed their masters from the College's preparatory side. Others who had arrived for the opening in 1888 were Francis John Bagshaw (future magistrate in the Orange River Colony), Charles Hamilton Bunbury (future captain in the Yorkshire Regiment), John Denison Paul, Edgar Tichborne Hibbert, John Dare Knight, Frank Jerome Sherrin, and the resoundingly-named Ernest Napoleon Eugene Mallet Vaughan, who also became — perhaps not altogether surprisingly — a Captain in the Grenadier Guards, and a veteran of the Boer War. Of this early disparate assembly, one of the briefest sojourns appears to have been that of James Aubrey Sidgreaves, who is mentioned as attending the Foundation only in 1889; his brother Reginald proceeded to the College until 1893, later serving with Cecil Rhodes in Matabeleland (now part of Zimbabwe), although died at some point before 1911. The most tragic names are Arthur à Beckett, who also joined in the academic year 1888–89, but died at the College in 1892 during his first year there, his brother drowning at Thornton Hall in the Wirral about the same time; and the aforementioned Gerald Woodlock, who died in 1903 in Denver, Colorado, where he was supposedly staying for health reasons. Five Woodlock boys studied at Beaumont over the years: Joseph, the youngest and a future Jesuit, is also present in this photograph, while his oldest brother, an authority on finance, became Editor of the Wall Street Journal. Further names from this little faded image may be tracked to the official records, from which an extraordinarily distinguished and fascinating clientele emerges: Francis Charles Devas (later a Jesuit), who wrote devotional poetry and a history of Beaumont College; Arthur Edward Silvertop, a future Commander in the Royal Navy (St John's had a enviable record of such ranks, but he would be a casualty of the Great War); Cyril Herbert Bretherton, future barrister; and Gilbert Pownall, the eminent artist who would design the majority of the mosaics in Westminster Cathedral. Pedro de Zulueta, composer and singer, and his brother Francis, Regius Professor of Civil Law at Oxford from 1919 (the first Catholic to hold the post) were also at St John's in 1888. 'Sykes' is Mark Sykes, later an M.P., Fellow of the

4 Although the identification has not been confirmed, initial research suggests that Eduardo was the son of Modesto Fresco and Wenceslada Guibara of Buenos Aires. He would presumably have returned there after preparatory schooling, if he did not attend naval college after all.

Elements II, 1899–1900. Given as Elements on the photograph, but elsewhere as Figures II (then the top year), which would seem more plausible. A tentative listing of names on reverse suggests the following: *Back row, left to right:* James Williams, Gordon [or Charlie] Gilbey, unidentified, Stephen Lyne Stevens, Luis d'Orleans [in fact, H.R.H. Prince Louis d'Orleans y Borbon, in his first year at St John's. He later presented the school with a most magnificent chalice, adorned with opals and Wedgwood silhouettes.] *Centre row:* Harry Gilbey, George Skinner, Mr Robert Dalrymple SJ, Gilbert Gerard, William Schutez. *Front row:* Maximilian Monk, Owen Lewis, William Munster, Angus Maitland, Robert Wilberforce.

Royal Geographical Society, and — along with Carlos Lumsden, future Sheriff of Norfolk — an army captain and another much-decorated veteran of the Boer War. Others present are Henry Charles Dickens, grandson of the novelist, who proceeded to Trinity Hall, Cambridge, and became a barrister; his brother Gerald, a future Admiral; Henry Melhado and his brother Carlos, who represented British Honduras in London at the coronation of George V; and Giles Gilbert Scott, who, at the age of 22, saw off more than a hundred other architects to produce the winning design for Liverpool Cathedral.[5] A photograph of senior boys from the following academic year includes Robert Wilberforce (later CBE), great-grandson of the anti-slavery campaigner William Wilberforce. He enjoyed a long and distinguished career in the diplomatic service, becoming the first full-time overseas information officer employed by the British Government; in 1988, he and St John's both celebrated their centenaries. These illustrious names are testament not only to the elevated position held by the College in its oft-repeated claim to educate the sons of Catholic gentlemen, but also the firm expectation placed in its new junior department that such an approach would be soundly maintained.

5 Hoy states (ibid, 4–7) that Gilbert Scott and his brother Adrian — also an architect — arrived in 1891 and 1892 respectively, but these were the years of their entering the College, not St John's. They together designed the Beaumont war memorial. As with Bentley at St John's, Giles Scott designed everything in the new cathedral down to the smallest detail, but it was not completed until 1978, nearly twenty years after his death. His later work included the Chapel at Charterhouse School, and the iconic K2 and K3 red telephone kiosks.

St John's, 1902.

Adrian [Gilbert Scott] used to say that when his father sent him and his brother to St John's he said he was not expecting spectacular results as he realised they had not a brain between them: but he was sure that if they could spend a few of their formative years in that beautiful little school built by his friend Bentley, they could not fail to imbibe the elements of civilisation and culture.[6]

6 Ibid.

7 *The Beaumont Review*, no. XXXIII (June 1902), 369. As mentioned above, the College in question is not Beaumont, but the Royal Naval College, initially at Dartmouth, and then Osborne on its opening in 1903. The cover of this edition of the *Review* is given as *Coronation Number* June 1902, but the serious illness of Edward VII (perityphlitis) caused the ceremony to be postponed until August. As this date was out of term, St John's and Beaumont celebrated the occasion in October, when it is reported that two brilliant electric bulbs, each of 600 candle power, shone in homage from St John's tower, and were visible from the private apartments of Windsor Castle.

There are about twenty-three new boys here this term [July 1902]. There is no Figures now but a Preliminary Navy Class preparing for the Navy Class at the College.[7]

The uniform, a small version of adult dress, as were nearly all children's formal clothes at the time, was appropriately sombre: grey trousers, white shirt with Eton collar, black waistcoat and high-cut jacket. The school's colours of chocolate brown, dark blue and light blue — symbolizing earth, sea and sky, as traversed and witnessed by St Stanislaus during his pilgrimages — were similarly borrowed from Beaumont College, who had adopted them in 1886 to replace their original cricket colours of black and white stripes, and as single colours for three Houses, named after Rectors. From 1906 the colours for cricket at the College were changed to green and white, so as to be the same as those used for football and boating,[8] but the St John's cricket cap was purple and cream: a distinctive choice, if not entirely logical.[9]

The boys' surroundings were scarcely luxurious, but clean, functional, and unpretentious. The boarding cubicles were based on those at the College, while a postcard of the washroom — an area still immediately recognisable — displays the marble and the mirrors, all designer-made for the occupants. Fixtures and fittings cannot always be dated with certainty, although a fascinating and copiously detailed inventory[10] of June 1931 records everything, down to the glue-pot in the workshop; and many of these items, particularly furnishings and religious artefacts, date to the earliest days of the School, so it is worth examining the document at this point. A tangible atmosphere of decorum is evoked by the entry for the preparatory classroom, including 'Oak Master's desk with shaped and panelled front mounted on deal platform', together with 'Fourteen oak desks with rising tops and folding seats attached', working arrangements that were reflected in the majority of classrooms.

*Top:* Cricket cap.

*Above:* Blazer badge for the Rugby XV.

*Far left*: Replica uniform, as worn in 1892.

*Left:* Joe Bowman shaking hands over the centuries.

8 *The Beaumont Review*, no. XLVII (June 1906), 371

9 The exact date of this item has not yet been ascertained: the caps from the 1930s were of a different design, as were the main school caps. Straw hats bearing the school colours were worn in the summer months.

10 Gurr Johns & Co. Ltd. *St John's Old Windsor: Inventory & valuation of the contents of St John's, Beaumont College.* [London]: Gurr Johns & Co. (1931).

Photocards, undated.

In the refectory ... the oak tables, octagonal and oblong in form, with simply turned pillar legs, are models of strength and simplicity ... Furniture, silver and china ware, indeed practically all the original furnishings of the school, were Bentley's personal choice, selected or designed with the same regard to harmony and fitness.[11]

St John's was a modest establishment, yet provided with china, glass and cutlery out of all proportion to its size, perhaps to allow for joint celebrations with its parent body. There were four hundred cups and saucers in plain white china alone, three hundred and ninety-six crested plates, and an enormous array of decorated items. The boys' refectory held one hundred and fifty-four teaspoons, with an additional thirty-eight in the community refectory; but the hoard of spare plate in Fr Hill's room contained a further two hundred and twenty-four of them, not to mention thirty-two more in the boys' infirmary, which would surely have sufficed for even the most bountiful feast.

By the time this inventory was compiled, the tiger in the entrance hall had migrated to the second parlour, where it languished along with a leopard of similarly resigned condition, and a statue of Mozart. As if in mitigation, the Playroom was host to a stuffed badger, six stuffed birds and a case of Indian moths (total value £4.0.0, no less); although, as now, it also housed a grand piano[12], two billiard tables, chess, table tennis, and a quantity of other games. Other sports equipment included two punch balls, some thirty-four pairs of dumb-bells (wood and iron), about ten sets of boxing gloves, seventy cricket balls, six Bridge tables and thirteen fencing foils, but only seven masks. Among the hotly-contested silverware were several trophies that have since become casualties of rubric, fashion or

11 L'Hôpital, ibid, 513

12 There were four other pianos scattered around the school at the time of the inventory, all upright models, and probably none of great merit.

St. Johns Beaumont, Old Windsor. Washing Place.

Photocard, undated.

educational approach, such as prizes for quarter-mile and hurdles, The Hon. Mrs Craven's Challenge Cup, and the Inter-Class Relay Race Challenge, for which the award was an embossed Chinese bowl with dragon decoration. There is no mention of certain esoteric items that had a revered place in the Playroom in the early years of the century, such as samples of ore from mines in Chile[13], and a substantial assembly of rare birds' nests and eggs.[14] Collecting such was then regarded as a perfectly respectable hobby.

Engravings, etchings, photographs and prints were plentiful, the subjects usually being ecclesiastical buildings or rural scenes, although the Hall boasted an oil of St Stanislaus by an unnamed executant.[15] The chapel gallery housed one of the most expensive individual items: a large American reed organ by Estey, with two manuals and fifteen stops, valued at £75. There were twenty-four richly-embroidered sets of silk and damask vestments in all seasonal colours, including black and old rose, together with several altar frontals, copes and stoles of similar opulence, and thirty-eight choristers' cassocks (twenty-six purple, twelve crimson). The boys' linen supply encompassed two hundred and sixty-nine cotton sheets, and one hundred and thirty-nine pillow cases, their combined personal wardrobes and possessions amounting to £2,960. Solemn medical listings enumerate two copper Alformant lamps for disinfecting rooms, five gargling mugs, a cylinder of oxygen, and a

13 *The Beaumont Review*, no. XL (July 1904), 395

14 Ibid., 405

15 No longer in situ. The refectory pictures were replaced in 1949: see *The Beaumont Review*, vol. XXII, no. 171 (July 1949), 293

bronchitis kettle, all stark reminders that school life could be hard and sometimes tragically short. Epidemics of measles, mumps, influenza and chickenpox were all too common. One prevented most of the School from witnessing the Coronation celebrations in 1937, another lingered through almost the whole of the Easter term of 1950, and some records are harrowing. Two ten-year-olds, Roger Anthony Molyneux, and Teddy Austin, died in 1902 and 1928 respectively, both as a result of unnamed illnesses. Molyneux, one of four choristers in the tiny choir, succumbed shortly after his first Communion. He was particularly dear to the community, his death and manner of passing inspiring panegyrics of greatly affectionate tributes, poetical and otherwise. Alfred Byrne died in 1915, aged nine, as a result of intensely painful complications following an operation for appendicitis, while Charles Hasslacker and Henry Bedingfield expired within a few days of each other in 1917, victims of an earlier epidemic of measles and pneumonia that struck at half the school. The necessity to trust in the slow work of God through periods of instability and grief must have sustained the community through dark days when pupils and friends were lost in heart-breaking circumstances.

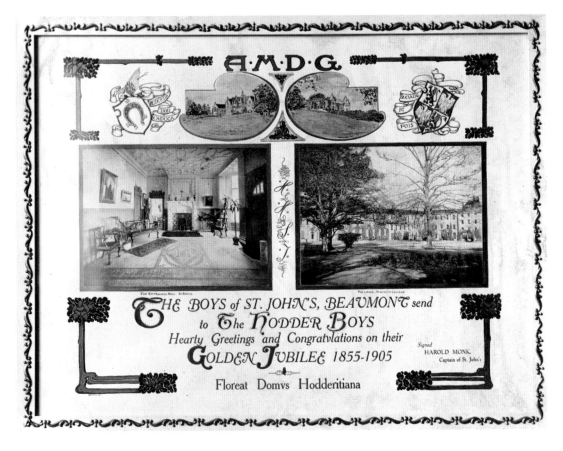

Presentation to Hodder Place, 1905.

His knowledge rules, His strength defends, His love doth cherish all;
His birth our joy, His life our light, His death our end of thrall ...
Almighty Babe, whose tender arms can force all foes to fly,
Correct my faults, protect my life, direct me when I die!

from *A Child My Choice*
Robert Southwell SJ (1561–1595)

By December 1904, there were fifty-six boys at the school. The following year, Beaumont's preparatory department, Hodder Place, celebrated its Golden Jubilee, and was presented with a large framed print showing the entrance hall at St John's and a view of the College.[16] A detailed account of the intensive daily timetable at St John's in that year is given by one F. Munster of Elements I.[17] A formal approach and thorough individual preparation were clearly the order of the long day, half-holidays and an hour's break in the afternoon being balanced by 'night schools' until 7:30 p.m. Yet, despite the concentrated hours, how little has changed in a century.

16 From earliest days, strong links were maintained with other Jesuit schools, notably Stonyhurst, which would receive most of the pupils from Beaumont College at its closure in 1965, as well as accepting responsibility for St John's. Following the demise of Hodder Place itself in 1970, the name was resurrected in 2004 as Stonyhurst's new pre-preparatory department.

17 *The Beaumont Review*, no. XLIII (May 1905), 184. F. Munster does not appear in the *Beaumont Lists* but John F. Munster does; if they are the same individual, it is curious that both names appear under separate articles on adjacent pages of the *Review*. There were certainly two generations of this family at Beaumont: two sets of brothers named John and William. The second William Munster appears in the front row of the earlier photograph of Elements II, 1899–1900: he proceeded to Stonyhurst, New College, Oxford, and then studied in Rome before joining the London Oratory. J.F. Munster became a Lieutenant, but was killed in World War I.

96. Study Hall, St. John's, Beaumont College.

Photocard, undated.

Clap! Clap! Clap! the signal to get up. A few snores, a few groans, and an assortment of words are heard as the sleepy boys tumble out of bed with their bed clothes on top of them. After they have disentangled themselves from their bed-clothes (which takes a few minutes), they find that they are rather late and dress so quickly that when they are dressed there is still about five minutes before they have to go down to chapel. But it suddenly dawns on them that they have forgotten to wash. More words, jugs broken, etc. When they have to go down to Chapel they are only brushing their hair. After that they go down to Mass. Then comes breakfast — meat, tea, coffee, toast, etc. After we have refreshed our inner man we go into the Study Hall at half-past eight and study hard, without exception, till half-past nine. We then go into our class room till twenty minutes to eleven. By that time we have been working so hard that we need a little fresh air, so we are let loose into the playground till eleven o'clock. At eleven o'clock we come in again and go into the playroom, where our letters are given to us. We go back into class at a quarter past eleven for arithmetic schools, though we do not necessarily study arithmetic. At a quarter to one we go up to our dormitories to make ourselves look respectable for dinner. When one o'clock strikes we go into the Refectory for dinner till a quarter to two when we go into the playground till a quarter to three. At three o'clock we go into the Study Hall for our afternoon studies till half past three. Then we go into class till five o'clock. After that we go into the playroom till half-past five, and after that we move on to the Refectory and have tea. But on half holidays we come in from the playground at a quarter past two, and go into the playroom till half past two. At half past two we go into the Study Hall and are allowed to read our books there till half past three. The half holidays are Tuesdays and Thursdays, but on Tuesdays those who learn drawing have their drawing class from a quarter to three till half-past three. On Thursdays the boxing class takes place from half-past two till half-past three. At half-past three we have a football match till about a quarter to five and then we go into the playroom till a quarter past five, when we go into the Refectory and enjoy tea till six o'clock. Then we move on to the Chapel till a quarter past six to pay a little visit, during that time we generally say our rosaries. At a quarter past six till half-past seven we have night schools, afterwards we have our supper till ten minutes to eight. When we have finished our supper we either go to the playroom or if we want to read or study we go to the Study Hall. At half-past eight we move on to the Chapel and say our night prayers. After they are finished we go up to our dormitories and go to bed. At about nine o'clock the lights are put out.

The average diet appears to have been fulfilling, if unexciting; and while extra fare at the very modest supper was considered unnecessary by the authorities — they had, after all, provided a most substantial breakfast, as well as bread and soup at morning break, followed by beer and two courses of meat at lunch — a somewhat grudging conciliation allowed the additional provision of hampers 'on the understanding that their contents are consumed during meals.' Later updating of the prospectus saw little change: 'Parents may visit their boys on Saturdays only from 12/30 until 5.20 ... No eatables from home of any kind are allowed ... Boys are never allowed to use the telephone'. However, life was not all routine, and was punctuated by a variety of high days and holidays. St John's has celebrated Shrove Tuesday in more or less extravagant fashion since its earliest days, log books usually noting that proceedings began with a Long Sleep, and that there was no work after mid-morning. A dramatic production usually featured, and two farces were presented that day in 1892: *Taming a Tiger* and *Fish out of Water,* complete with piano solos as overture and interlude. One of the earliest mentions of outlandish attire on this occasion is the Carnival and Fancy-Dress Ball of 1948 to raise money for foreign missions; the tradition of costumes on Shrove Tuesday is still maintained at the time of writing.

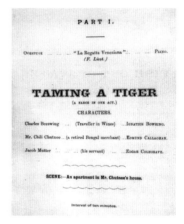

*Top*: Boarder's cubicle, undated.

*Above*: Programme for Shrovetide, 1892.

St John's, 1906.

Postcards dated 9 July 1910, and 21 July 1910, from Edgar Spence to Mrs Spence.

St John's holds three postcards from 1910, written by Edgar Spence, son of the English Consul General at Trieste, Austria. Edgar had joined the school in September of the previous year. These correspondences form some of the earliest first-hand accounts of everyday life at the school: in holding them, a tactile portal opens into history. The example to his father, dated 5 May, is in English, while the remaining two cards, dated 9 July and 21 July, are in Italian and addressed simply to 'Mrs Spence' at the same address, or at 7 Via S. Nicolo, Trieste. All three cards are touching in their discussion of matters not far removed from the concerns of much more recent generations, the vitally important domestic matters pertaining to a schoolboy: work, money, personal collections, the weather, his teachers, and the craved closeness of home.

Dear Father,
Many thanks for the newspaper. I had already seen it. The Lord Mayor of London[18] came to Beaumont on the 3rd, and after to St John's, as he is an old Beaumont boy. To-day is a whole holiday but it is raining so we can't play cricket. I collect cigarette pictures, so if you have any please keep them for me. Much love from your son, Edgar.

Dearest Mama,
Miss Hancock has written to me to ask if I can resend the geography but I do not know her address so I am unable to reply. Can you tell her that I will resend the geography when I have finished this competition which will be in 2 weeks. G in the meantime can do Latin which will be much more useful for school. Please can you send me the senior geography. I hope that you are well as am I. Lots of kisses from your Edgar.

18 Sir John Stuart Knill (1886–1973), third Baronet of The Grove, Blackheath, Kent, was Lord Mayor from 1909–1910. His father, also Sir John Stuart Knill (1856–1934), was also Lord Mayor from 1892–1893, the first Roman Catholic to hold this office since the Reformation. Shortly after succeeding to the title in 1934, the third Baronet lost not only his Hertfordshire estate but his entire fortune, at one point taking a job as a road sweeper (one trusts that he was at least partly sustained by his family motto, *Nil desperandum*); but the saintly fourth name of his second child, Gyles Braoze Hamish Stanislas Stuart Knill, is surely testimony to his father's early years at Beaumont.

St John's, 1911 – possibly including Edgar Spence.

Dearest Mama,
Many thanks for your letter. I am thinking of writing to Mr Chaplin and Giaccia etc. The £1 has not arrived. The work from trofano will not fit in my suitcase so I shall have to take it by hand. Aunt Bessie writes that I must go to her. I will let you know what Father Phaeler tells me when I arrive (I mean on the idea of sending G to school) and it is better not to write to him. Nothing to report from this end. Many kisses from your Edgar. P.S. Here, the exams are all this week, 2 every day so it won't shock you if I don't manage to write to you until I am at Aunt Bessie's.[19]

St John's Silver Jubilee, celebrated in 1913, was a relatively small-scale affair — partly because of the recent major celebrations in 1911 for the College's Golden anniversary — although events nonetheless appear to have been lively enough, with a large party, services and a sports day. At some point around this time, a series of postcard views of Beaumont College and St John's was produced by Fr A Tempest, one of the Jesuit scholastics, some of which appear in this volume.[20] However, political storm-clouds were gathering, and the calm and assured lives of the boys were about to be overtaken by cataclysmic events.

19 Translations by Daniela Harwood and Paola Bright. As a 'trofano' is an ugly-looking fish from the Adriatic, it is presumed that Edgar was complaining about the quantity of homework set by an unfavoured master.

20 Published by Spearman's of Eton, and advertised in *The Beaumont Review*, no. LXXVIII (March 1914). Fr Tempest joined the Community in 1909 and was still on the staff of St John's in 1945. The archive copies are possibly part of the legacy of H. Richard Gilbey, who, in 1961, presented 'some snaps of St John's in 1911'. See *The Beaumont Review*, vol. XXIX, no. 201 (October 1961), 142

# 3. World War I

The little boys of long ago looked out across the trees
To where the Royal Standard floats on Royal Windsor's height,
When trouble gathered never hearts more loyal rose than these
In answer to the call that bade the sons of Empire fight.
Our brothers from St John's serve in the army of the King,
Our brothers in the King's ships on the high seas ride
To every sphere of British life our grown-up brothers bring
The noble service that is born of true and lawful pride.[1]

The fortunes of war, meticulously chronicled in successive issues of *The Beaumont Review*, tell a familiar tale of battles, medals, and mentions in despatches, while the faith, trust and memories of those left behind are still immensely moving one hundred years on. Reports focus on the great responsibilities that now rested on such young shoulders, but also reflect on happier days, before self-sacrifice and patriotic duty flowered among this lost generation, and swept away their world for ever. Particular tragedies included Charles Anthony Dalglish (Captain, The Black Watch), who died of wounds on 9 September 1914, just over five weeks into the War. His family later gave the stained glass windows in the chapel to his memory; his brother was Robin Campsie Dalglish (shown here). Raymond John Purcell (Captain, King's Rifle Corps), was wounded in 1914 and mentioned in despatches, his gallantry well-documented.

'[Lieutenant R. J. Purcell] left Southampton on August 12 [1914] with the Second Brigade, First Division. He has been fighting continuously since then, having been often in the trenches for more than five days at a time. From a letter written Oct. 6 he mentions that his machine gun had killed two hundred Germans, and that he had accounted for fifteen with his own hand. On the 4th his horse was shot under him — he has been acting as assistant adjutant. He rescued a wounded man who was lying between the respective firing lines and carried him back out of danger.'

*Opposite, clockwise from left:* Robin Campsie Dalgish (1880–1934). Studio portrait, 13 October 1890. Beaumont College 1890–93. Lieutenant, RN.

Raymond John Purcell. Studio portrait, 1896. Beaumont College 1875–1902, then Christ Church, Oxford. Captain, 4th Batt. King's Royal Rifle Corps. Wounded 1934, mentioned in despatches.

Malcolm and Cuthbert Hay. Signed studio double portrait, 1892 (photographed 1891). Malcolm: Major, Gordon Highlanders. Wounded 1914, mentioned in despatches. Cuthbert: 3rd Gordons. Wounded twice. Both attended Beaumont College 1891–97, overlapping with their relations mentioned above, who were some of the earliest St John's boys.

1 F.C.D. [Francis Charles Devas], from 'St John's Jubilee', *The Beaumont Review*, no. LXXVI (July 1913), 1

Rudiments, 1914–15. Fr Duffy is in the centre; a few other names are annotated on the reverse. Fourth from left on the back row is an early casualty: 'José Bush RIP.'

A later letter states that the machine gun referred to above was captured by Purcell himself from the German trenches.[2] Similar exploits are reported of Malcolm Hay (Major, Gordon Highlanders) and his brother Cuthbert (Third Gordons).

Lieut. [Malcolm] Hay was in the trenches at the battle of the Marne, where he was shot through the head [as he stood up] at 4 p.m. on 26 August [1914], and left for dead behind the trenches when his battalion retired; but at 10 a.m. next day he was found by the French and carried into the village of Caudry, whence he was sent to hospital at Cambrai. At the beginning of [1915] he was sent to Wurzburg in Bavaria, and finally in February was allowed to return to England.

Captain Cuthbert Hay … was again wounded at Neuve Chapelle, losing the sight of his right eye. He is now on duty at the Barracks, Aberdeen.[3]

2 Letter from Mrs Purcell [identity not ascertained], quoted in *The Beaumont Review*, no. LXXXI (November 1914), 6

3 *The Beaumont Review*, no. LXXXV (December 1915), 143

| Date recd 1918 | Intention | Stpd | Date said 1918 | By whom | Date recd 1918 | Intention | Stpd | Date said 1918 | By whom |
|---|---|---|---|---|---|---|---|---|---|
| Jan: 31 | A deceased father R.I.P. | 5/- | Feb. 3 | G. Sexton | June 5 | Jim Gudgeon's safe return. | 2/6 | June 7 | G. Sexton |
| Feb: 20 | Bevan Harold (O.B.) | " | " 20 | " | " 5 | Will | " | " 9 | " |
| " 22 | For those dying alone on the battlefield | 5/- | " 26 | " | " 10 | Sister Columba | " | " 14 | " |
| " 27 | F. & L. Carral's father R.I.P (lately dead) | 5/- | " 28 | " | " 15 | Ad intent: dantis (in hon. of the Precious Blood) | " | " 21 | " |
| " 28 | do. | 2/6 | Mar. 1 | " | " - | do | " | " 23 | " |
| Mar: 1 | Adrian Green Armitage's recovery | 5/- | " 3 | " | " 20 | Ad mentem donantis. | " | " 24 | " |
| " 30 | Grace Carling | 2/6 | Apl. 1 | " | | Emma Eames | " | " 25 | " |
| " 31 | An annivers-ary R.I.P. | " | " 2 | " | | Annie Green R.I.P. | " | " 26 | " |
| Apl: 9 | G. E. Noble (anniv y:) | " | " 12 | " | " - | Miriam Barton | " | " 27 | " |
| " .. | do. | 5/- | " 13 | " | " 25 | Safety of Mr. Winstanley's brother. | 5/- | " 30 | " |
| " 28 | Richard Raymond-Barker | 2/6 | " 29 | " | " 29 | Geoffrey Callaghan's safe return. | 2/6 | July 1 | " |
| " - | A special intention | 5/- | " 30 | " | | do. | " | " 2 | " |
| May 11 | Will Gudgeon's safe return | 2/6 | May 14 | " | " 30 | Sergt. Leo MacKinnon R.I.P. | " | " 3 | " |
| " .. | Jim | 2/6 | " 15 | " | | Mary Callaghan | " | " 4 | " |
| " 18 | Jim | | " 20 | " | | Richard Barry O'Brien | " | " 5 | " |
| " - | | | " 21 | " | | Private Intention | " | " 7 | " |
| " 27 | Tom Tolhurst's success in Exam. | 5/- | " 29 | " | July 5 | Miriam Barton | " | " 8 | " |
| " 29 | A Special intention. | 2/6 | June 2 | " | | do. | " | " 9 | " |
| June 2 | Miriam Barton R.I.P. | 2/6 | " 5 | " | | do. | " | " 10 | " |
| " - | do. | | " 6 | " | | do. | " | " 11 | " |

The St John's *Codex Missarum* from 1918 records Masses offered 'For those dying alone on the battlefield', and for the safe return of those hundreds who were away. As the great conflict drew slowly to a close, St John's gave thanks and continued quietly about its daily business, as well as improving and preserving its fabric. One addition was a new Lady Shrine, notably Italianate in design, although L'Hôpital was most unhappy about it. She may have considered that the design spoiled the simplicity of her father's conception, in which case the obscuring of the windows cannot have improved her opinion.[4] Unfortunately for her, she appears to have been a comparatively lone voice, as the shrine proved immediately popular.

On the Feast of Our Lady of Lourdes we had the opening of the new Lady Shrine which Fr. Green built and paved with white marble ... The procession consisted of the three Satelites, the boys and four banner bearers, the statue carriers, the choir, the community and the parents. At the Shrine, Father Rector, who had kindly come up, read an Act of Consecration to Our Lady, which we repeated

St John's *Codex Missarum*, 1918–1954.

4 L'Hôpital, ibid., 512. While the shrine does not appear on Bentley's plan (p. 10), the exterior gives no indication that the alcove is anything other than contemporary with the rest of the cloister, although the lantern turret is probably more recent. The boys would kneel at the shrine (or the wall) for evening prayers, including the *Salve Regina*, before repairing to their dormitories via the 'night stairs' opposite.

ST JOHNS, BEAUMONT CHAPEL, ARMISTICE DAY, NOV: 11TH 1918

*Top:* Lady Shrine.

*Above:* Memorial plaque to Dermot Gogarty.

*Right:* Photocard, *c.*1918.

after him. When we got back to the Chapel we had Solemn Benediction, and after that a hymn to Our Lady. The altar was decorated with an extra blaze of candles and an extra amount of flowers. This day was considered one of the finest and greatest days of the whole term.[5]

Latterly, with the cloister itself being rarely used, the shrine has continued to be a much-venerated part of the School, and the focus of many prayers and intentions; not least the moving lines of James Scholes, inscribed on the prayer desk given by the Rudiments boys of 2005–2006 in memory of Dermot St John Gogarty.

On November 11th (lovely day!) the Germans signed the Armistice. Brother Ellingworth hoisted the Union Jack from the Clock Tower and the Chapel was bedecked with flags. In the evening we were freed from Night Studies and had a thanksgiving service for the peace that had come upon the world once more. At the end of Benediction we all stood up and sang 'God Save the King.'[6]

Æterna non Caduca:
Blaze that motto on the brass!
For they have changed deciduous days
For years that do not pass.[7]

5 *The Beaumont Review*, no. XCIII (April 1918), 373. A separate Grotto of Our Lady of Lourdes was created in 1923 by Bro. Ellingworth. It has not survived, but photographic evidence suggests it was a fairly modest edifice.

6 *The Beaumont Review*, no. XCV (April 1919), 455

7 Jackson, Arthur Austin, from 'Our Dead'. *The Beaumont Review*, no. XXXIII (October 1902), 374.

*Trench Warfare* by Astemir
Azhakhov. Acrylic on canvas,
2014.

Details of ceiling in entrance hall.

# 4. Respite and Consolidation

*Opposite: Alice in Wonderland,* 1938. The Duchess (Paul Leonard), Alice (John Mathews) and the Mock Turtle (Alexandre Waterkeyn). 1938 was the fortieth anniversary of Carroll's death.

1 Dixon, T. J., 'Music Notes', *The Beaumont Review*, no. XLIV (August 1905), 242. This was modest indeed, comprising violin, clarion (high trumpet), and piano duet; but Dixon's report that 'It is the first time that there has ever been anything of that sort at St John's' is misleading, and seems to refer only to an ensemble. The previous year, Cecil Wegg-Prosser had enthused, 'The music at St John's is very good, and our concerts have been a great success. Most boys learn the piano, some learn the violin, and some singing. One learns the cello and I learn the harmonium, which is indeed a very interesting instrument.' See *The Beaumont Review*, no. XXXIX (March 1904), 332. Wegg-Prosser became a Sub-Lieutenant, but was a casualty of World War I.

2 See *The Beaumont Review*, vol. XVIII, no. 147 (July 1936), 805; and Prefect's Log, January 1942ff, ibid. Dramas of a similar nature at Christmas and Easter were given in 1959 and 1960 under the auspices of Mr O'Mahoney, SJ (a Jesuit scholastic who later moved to Beaumont College), with Passion performances on Palm Sunday 1964 under Fr Dunphy, and most recently at Easter 1971.

3 Reviewed in *The Stage*, quoted in *The Beaumont Review*, vol. XIX, no. 153 (July 1938), 395

4 Ibid.

Archive holdings for the inter-war years at St John's are comparatively plentiful, although occasionally rather bland: even many of the individual portraits seem to lack the character that was captured during the more protracted photographic sessions of earlier generations. The Prefect's Log for 1933–34 amusingly records that Firework Day was preceded earlier in the month by a 'Mass Against Fire', while other details therein are highly evocative of a departed age, such as the menu for High Tea (sardines on toast), or annotated fixture lists recalling past sporting triumphs.

It is also clear that drama and music remained particularly strong, and had developed beyond all measure since the first mention of a tiny orchestra in 1905.[1] The celebrations for many feast days often included a concert or play of some description, and a variety of sketches, solos, classics, burlesques and pantomimes punctuated the terms. A small stage for such events was created in 1919 at one end of Study Hall. In 1935, the triumph of a home-grown nativity drama entitled *The Prince of Peace* (mostly *tableaux vivants*, interspersed with carols by Holst, Boughton, Terry and others), led indirectly to a dramatic mime of the Passion presented in chapel three years later, that was pronounced 'very very successful.'[2] The open-air production of *Alice in Wonderland* to celebrate the School's Golden Jubilee in 1938 was a major event that attracted the enthusiastic attention of *The Stage*, special note being given to Alexandre Waterkeyn as the Mock Turtle, 'who as part of an excellent performance, with ready wit turned the untimely explosion of sundry balloons to account to emphasize his mock sorrow'.[3]

Those who have known something of the difficulties of outdoor performance can admire the skill of these young actors. They had learnt to speak slowly, with correct and natural diction, which made their words heard with ease … In several cases it was remarkable to find children acting with such ease and freedom. Staged in a rose garden surrounded with trees, the setting gave scope for some ingenious and delightful touches. Alice disappearing through an improvised rabbit-hole, a Cheshire Cat grinning high up in its native tree and gardeners painting roses growing in a rose bed, added charm and realism to an attractive scene.[4]

A later presentation that year consisted of scenes from A. A. Milne's *Make-Believe*, a truncated account of the play that focussed on the second story of the original three, 'Oliver's Island'. A typical pantomime was *Cinderella* of Christmas 1939, with topical names of characters, such as Lord N. Chamberlain [Prime Minister], the two ugly sisters Ovaltine and Kiaora [beverages] and Mr Willis of Freeman, Hardy & Willis [footwear retailers]. The Fairy Godmother's adversary, the Demon King, was evidently a favourite, since he also materialised in *Robinson Crusoe* from 1945, on which occasion the actor was the future distinguished organist Nicholas Danby. Greater maturity was showcased when the school emulated Beaumont College by performing scenes from Shakespeare, notably *Henry V* in 1955, an excerpt from *The Merchant of Venice* in 1963, and the 'Pyramus and Thisby' play from *A Midsummer Night's Dream* in 1966. All parts, male and female, were taken by the boys. When it is remembered that there were well under one hundred pupils in the School during these years, it is clear that not only an immense versatility was present, but also a fervent *esprit de corps*.

*Left:* Scene from the 1971 production of *A Mime of the Passion*.

*Above: Cinderella,* Christmas 1939. Derek Duncombe (Fairy Godmother), John Collier (Demon King).

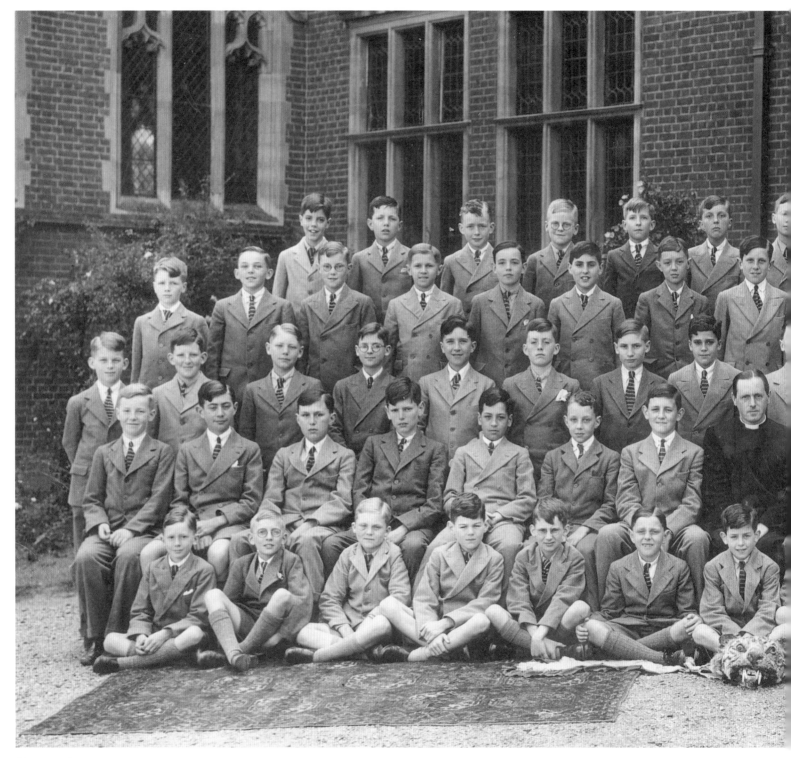

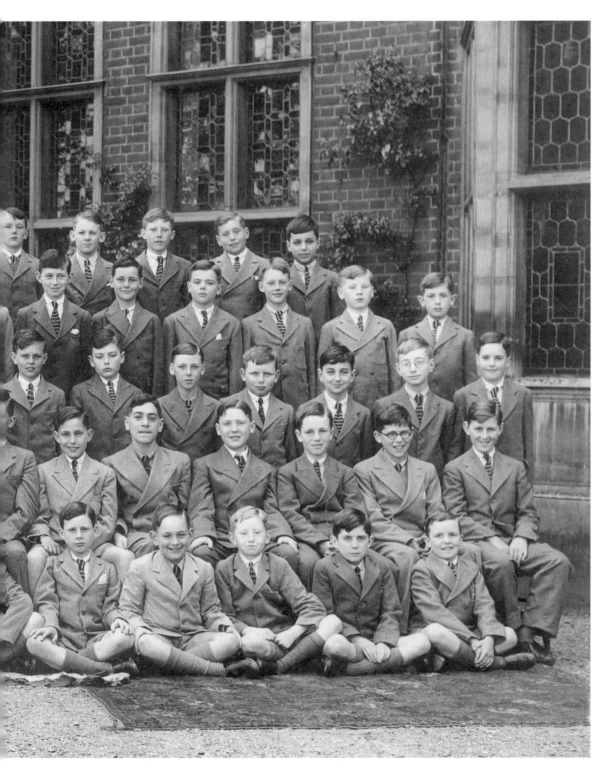

St John's, 1935; together with the last-known appearance of the exhausted tiger from the entrance hall. While he may have endured many such indignities, it is not improbable that he was at least partially the inspiration for the Animal house still surviving.

# 5. Scouts and activities

As mentioned above, pupils at Beaumont College prior to World War II were divided into three Houses: Eccles (the first Rector), O'Hare (the builder of St John's), and Heathcote (the first Old Beaumont boy to become Rector). However, the usual practice in Jesuit education employed the 'Line' system of horizontal 'Playrooms' in year groups.[1] In addition, each class was divided into 'Romans' or 'Carthaginians' who, led by their Imperatores, competed against each other, earning points for academic and personal progress. This nomenclature may be traced to the earliest Jesuit foundations of 1548, and is echoed in the first verse of *Carmen Beaumontanum*:

> Etsi mox pugnavimus
> Iam condamus enses,
> Seu Romani fuimus
> Seu Carthaginenses.[2]

St John's also followed this system, competitions and teams being organized horizontally by year, and for many decades there were no Houses at the school at all. Prime importance was given to academic standing in each class through individual effort in exams, recognized by the Imperatores' medals that were presented at the beginning of term to acknowledge achievement and leadership.[3] Well after the House system had become firmly established, these suitably military decorations, with an image of the Blessed Virgin on the obverse, were retained for years as independent stimuli to progress: boys may be seen proudly wearing them in photos of the Queen's visit in 1961. Almost the only large-scale extra-curricular activity was Scouting, which appears to have begun at St John's in the 1920s, and long maintained an enthusiastic following, continuing at Beaumont College from 1941. There still hangs in the Sacristy an unsigned illustration in watercolour and pencil, that emphasizes the devout nature of the movement, together with the central intention to find God in all times and seasons. It probably dates from the late 1950s, and although modern eyes may consider it a little saccharine, it is more than competent, and recalls the characterful work of Treyer Evans (1889–1958) in such volumes as *The Golden Book of Carols*.[4]

*Opposite:* Campfire in the woods, undated.

1 The term 'Lines' derives from the fact that the boys assembled on painted lines in the playground before marching into class, as they still do at Wimbledon College (from which also probably stems the marching groups of competitors on lines at St John's Sports' Day). The Ascensio Scholarum was the act of moving up to higher forms each year, a ceremony that also took place at St John's. The author is indebted to Fr Adrian Porter SJ for for his clarification of this matter.

2 'Even though we fought recently/ Let us put away our swords/Whether we were Romans/Or Carthaginians'. (Translation by Mark Walker.) The divisions of Romans and Carthaginians were also employed at St John's, although by 1925 it was hinted that the names had become somewhat jaded. See *The Beaumont Review*, no. CXIII (April 1925), 457.

3 For example, see typewritten timetables for Christmas Term 1945, and Easter Term 1946, included in the Prefect's Log, January 1942ff., and published lists of awards, e.g. *The Beaumont Review*, vol. XXIII, no. 164 (April 1946). 'Distinctions' in school work are also mentioned occasionally, such achievements resulting in a plentiful supper.

4 London: Blandford Press (1948). It is presumed that the little painting was created by one of the staff; however, with no known provenance, it is quite possible that it was acquired elsewhere, and the personalised supplication added later.

St John's First Scout Troop —
14th Windsors, 1940.
*Back row:* Desmond Browning,
James Manley, George Du
Boulay, Michael Obolensky,
William Hammond, Ian
Douglas, Peter Low [later
SJ], Paul Warren, Darragh
Waterkeyn, Hugh Dowley.
*Centre row:* Alan Leakey,
Patrick Hickey, Desmond
Mahony, Derek Duncombe,
Richard Insoll, Peter Doyle.
*Front row:* Peter Pain, Michael
Rose, Anthony Motion,
John Collier. The original
photograph is annotated
on the reverse with names.
Evident errors have been
silently corrected but Michael
Rose does not appear in the
relevant lists, and is probably
James Rose, who is on the roll
for the following term. If so,
he must have been visiting
or else had joined the School
mid-way through the summer
term, which might explain why
he has no hat (although not
why Motion also lacks one).
Manley's name is spelt thus,
but also without the 'e' on
other occasions. Doyle, Motion
and Waterkeyn were the only
boys left from this group the
following term, although Du
Boulay, Low, Pain and Warren
had rejoined by summer 1941.

*Opposite right:* Display on
Sports Day, 1940.

Assorted hurdling.

St John's Scouts, 1960.

Scoutly devotion, artist unknown.

One of the earliest accounts of team-games at St John's is a report from 1919 that the boys had begun 'Ribbon Matches' in rugby (they had only received their first instruction in the sport the previous year), the school being divided into four groups, such as 'The Irish Guards' or 'The Beavers', each with a different coloured ribbon. Notwithstanding the piety of the foundation, it seems probable that exotic animals were considered more endearing to preparatory school boys than teams named after saints or martyrs. In 1921 the scout patrols were Otters, Tigers, Kangaroos, Owls and Lions.[5] They gave substantial displays at the annual sports' day, and possibly on other occasions. After the inevitable exodus of boys at the end of an academic year, the troops were re-founded to the comfortable maximum of twenty, anything greater quickly becoming unwieldy. It is from these years that the development of Animal Houses may be traced. Beginning with only Tigers and Yaks — no doubt because the relatively small number of boys in the School did not warrant further divisions — the two creatures are alleged to have metamorphosed quite simply from individual scout patrols, and were probably introduced by Fr Bernard Basset, under whose headmastership (1946–49) they certainly flourished.[6] The flags in extant photographs of the scouts give only tantalizing glimpses of the mascots, although one is undoubtedly that of the Bulldogs.

Following competitions, camps, manoeuvres and displays, came the great day of reckoning — what is now the Animal Count-Up — at which the prize was a Victory Walk and a special tea, during which the losers had to study. By April 1935, four beasts were in contest: Tigers, Yaks, Rhinos and Buffaloes (popularly known as 'Buffs').[7] In 1938 each boasted roughly sixteen boys, and competition became fierce, the reporter in *The Beaumont Review* writing that summer:

Though we have been divided up into Rhinos, Tigers, Yaks and Buffaloes for a long time now, we were never quite certain what a Yak was till the end of last term, when we all met in the finals of the Inter-Animal Rugby Competition and each team used Corner and Touch flags bearing a likeness of its own Animal. This term we all have bathing drawers with our own animals on and they look very smart indeed.[8]

5 L. Redmund Roche, *The Beaumont Review*, no. CIII (December 1921), 18

6 The author is indebted to Mr Ted Coyle for this information.

7 Report on Inter-Animal Cross Country, *The Beaumont Review*, vol. XVIII, no. 143 (April 1935), 555

8 *The Beaumont Review*, vol. XVIII, no. 144 (July 1935), 632

While personalised bathing drawers have been consigned to history, this does appear to mark the beginning of the distinctive Sports Day that still obtains at St John's, each Animal house processing to the Front Field, their respective banners held high. In 1940 the scout patrols had become Kingfishers, Hawks, Badgers and Bulldogs, each with roughly three or four boys,[9] while later subdivisions were named Panthers, Wolves, Squirrels, Stonechats, Kestrels, Woodpigeons, and — perhaps in memory of the House that was by then extinct — Rhinos. However, by autumn 1939, the Prefect's Log was largely concerned with marches and banners pertaining to much graver matters.

*Top:* Scout Troop, undated.

*Above:* Imperatores' Medals for Elements and Figures.

9 *The Beaumont Review*, vol. XX, no. 159 (July 1940), 292

East window of chapel.

*Opposite:* Detail above window on right of façade.

# 6. World War II

War was declared three weeks before the start of term, but little evacuation appears to have taken place. Many parents lived too far away to travel easily, were not encouraged to do so, and Windsor was then considered as safe as most places. In fact, many boys returned early, and (according to the Prefect's Log) 'romped around' for three weeks, living in the Infirmary; some twenty had returned by the start of term. A 'funk hole' was made in the cellar, and the boys held practice drills for escape there in case of need. Encamped in their relatively peaceful surroundings, life continued more or less as usual for a time, including a degree of Animal rivalry. An invaluable record from Christmas 1939 lists all the boys in the school by academic achievement, as well as by their Animal membership. In 1940 it was decided that three groups would be preferable, resulting in an announcement that the Rhinos had 'crowned a career of glory by an equally glorious sacrifice to public spirit and no longer exist. Their unabated vigour under other colours proved that their spirits were by no means quenched.'[1] Nonetheless, despite the gung-ho appearance of relative normality that was maintained, the Second World War visited upon the boys the hardships of rationing, some physical discomfort, and considerable mental strain. Two bombs near Wraysbury were the only near-misses throughout the conflict, but there were rockets and other dangers. Memories of lighter activities, such as raising rabbits in the playground, are set sharply against recollections of the Blitz:

> We began the term [September 1940] with the Blitzkrieg in full force over London. Stray 'planes and passing formations were certainly above us on many a night of the first half-term. Guns barked, bombs fell in the district, and some nights were spent in the shelter. One heavy bomb fell in the brothers' walk. St John's was not damaged at all. We say these things because we have heard of people who go about giving our parents undue worry and anxiety by putting our small share in the ordeal of London in a very untrue light. We sleep comfortably round the galleries, and feel very secure, for between us and the outside are two stout walls. Our sleep is not disturbed. The muffled flash of a lamp in the dead of night only adds to our sense of security, for we know that someone watches over us through every time of possible danger.[2]

1 *The Beaumont Review*, vol. XX, no. 158 (March 1940), 235

2 *The Beaumont Review*, vol. XX, no. 160 (December 1940), 370

## 1939

a.m.d.g.                                     Christmas Term.

War declared 3 weeks before the boys were due back.
One by one they came back early & just romped
about for 3 weeks, lived in Infirmary. There were
about 20 in the house by the beginning of term.
Ghost Storys at night by boys & scholastics
Funk Hole made in the cellar. Gym becomes shoe
place.    So far ( Oct. 22 ) 2 practices for going
there have been held.  Long sleep of 1 hour.
next day.

Since the Germans were losing so many planes, by the time we were at St John's the air-raids had been switched to the night time, and we could hear the German bombers passing overhead on their way to London ... [Later] the Germans launched the V1 and V2 rockets ... If it was a V1 one could hear the engine chugging overhead. When it suddenly stopped we knew it would start falling at angle of 45 degrees, so we dived under the nearest table and just waited for the explosion, hoping it wouldn't be on top of us. If it was a V2 we heard nothing since this was a rocket that climbed high before dropping. I well remember the night one fell on the Bells of Ouseley[3] and killed five people. During the daytime we had classes in the dormitories and slept at night in the downstairs galleries. But if the air-raid sirens went, we had to get up and take a blanket to the only two places where there were no windows: the steps leading down to the chapel and the passage and steps leading up to the infirmary. And there we tried without much success to sleep. One night a rocket fell between St John's and Beaumont on what used to be called the 'brothers walk'. The next day the summer term was brought to an abrupt end and we went home some two to three weeks early. This was a blessing since many of the masters had to do fire watching during the night with the result that they sometimes nodded off in the daytime classes ...[4]

3 Located on Straight Road, Windsor, it is now a Harvester restaurant.

4 MCJ [Michael Jurgens, at St John's from the Christmas term 1939 to the end of the Christmas term 1940], *St John's in Wartime* (n.d.). Typewritten script (St John's archive). These details are confirmed by the report in *The Beaumont Review*, vol. XX, no. 160 (December 1940), 370; and by similar recollections from Christopher Roberts (see below).

| A.M.D.G. | | | CHRISTMAS 1939 |
|---|---|---|---|
| **1st "30"** | | **2nd "30"** | |
| Mathew | Obolensky | Incledon | Cuddigan |
| Insoll | Scott | Pribram | Daubeny |
| Hoban | Collier | Bosanquet | Harvey |
| Mahony | Duggan | Du Boulay | M.Jurgens |
| Browning | Mearns | Low | W.Jurgens |
| Cahill | N.Caddell | Pain | Little |
| de Zulueta | Doyle,P.(R) | Burgess | Riddell |
| Dowley | de Burgh (T) | Doyle, F. | Southwell |
| Guillet | Agar-Hutton | Jackson | Whitehead. |
| Hickey | Douglas | McNaught | Roberts |
| Watson | Shelley | Lennard | Parkes |
| Keighley | Warren | Puech | |
| Leakey | Greenaway | R-Jones | |
| Leonard | Hammond | Waterkeyn | |
| O'Gorman | Lane | Wilcox | |
| Marr | Manley | R.Jurgens | |
| Meyer | Russell | de Stempel | |

| A.M.D.G. | ANIMALS | | Christmas 1939 |
|---|---|---|---|
| | BUFFALOES | RHINOS | TIGERS | Y.KS |
| Patron | Fr. Ferguson | Mr.Dunphy | Fr.Manning | Mr.Brown |
| Captain | Mathew | Browning | Hoban | de Zulueta |
| | Mahony | Obolensky | Insoll | Hickey |
| | Leonard | P.Doyle | Dowley | Keighley |
| | A-Hutton | F.Doyle | de Burgh | Meyer |
| | Incledon | Guillet | Collier | Shellry |
| | McNaught | Duggan | Hammond | Pain |
| | Pribram | Wilcox | Greenaway | Lane |
| | Burgess | N-Caddell | Leakey | R-Jones |
| | Russell | Low | Waterkeyn | Marr |
| | Riddell | Roberts | Watson | M.Jurgens |
| | Mearns | O'Gorman | Manley | Scott |
| | Douglas | Cahill | Warren | Little |
| | Du Boulay | Bosanquet | Motion | R.Jurgens |
| | Cuddigan | Jackson | Lennard | W.Jurgens |
| | Harvey | Southwell | Puech | de Stempel |
| | | Perkes | Laubeny | Whitehead |

L.D.S.

A candid group photo taken in the 'funk hole' during September 1940 shows Michael Obolensky (1926–1995), the grandson of Tsar Alexander III; the National Portrait Gallery holds eleven prints of him, taken between 1943 and 1946. The family fled Russia after the 1917 Revolution, and settled in England. Michael was the younger brother of Prince Alexander Obolensky, pilot and rugby player, who (as the Prefect's Log noted) was killed on 29 March 1940 at the age of 24, while landing his aircraft at the 'East Coast aerodrome', now Martlesham Heath, Suffolk. The War, as chronicled, encompasses international incidents ('Russia invades Finland'), weather reports ('Snow for weeks. Hardly ever able to move out') together with accounts of domestic matters, such as the Scouts' Play in the park, and various illnesses. During these uncertain years, precautions were as thorough as possible, boys being encouraged to ensure everything was in place in case of need: 'Gas masks on bed heads'. The boys also attempted to make some modest sacrifices for the war effort, adapting their clubs and pastimes accordingly. The Toy Club metamorphosed into a

*Above left:* Alan Fraser, Head Boy 1939–40.

*Above right:* St John's roll, Christmas 1939.

Standing fast. St John's, 1939.

SEPT. 22nd. 1942

7.00  Supper

Night Prayers,washing,bed.

(Gas_Masks on Bed Heads)

To-night......make sure you have a towel,soap,
 tooth-brush and paste,pyjamas and slippers
 before you go to bed. If you have not any of
 these things ask Mr.Dunphy NOW.

Jungle Club, encompassing such pursuits as animal welfare, model village building, nature walks, gardening and story reading; while in April 1942, the Prefect remarked dramatically and clearly with no little relief:

● Wednesday April 15th 1942
Super-Red Letter Day:
The Benedictine Sisters took over all the Domestic duties of St John's.
They are marvellous![5]

The nuns who ran the catering and housekeeping during these years were German. They had been interned in Southampton at the outbreak of war as they were en route to Germany from Africa, so began to leave St John's in 1947. Two long-serving successors were Rose Harley and Teresa Wells, who both arrived that year. Rose remained at St John's until 1963 with only two and half years' absence; Teresa left in 1965. Their records have been more than eclipsed by the remarkable tenure of housekeeper Mrs Maria Martin, who joined the staff in 1967 and is still serving at the time of writing.

The Buffaloes were still flourishing in 1943, but fairly soon afterwards they were also allowed to become extinct, and from the following year rivalry again existed only between Tigers and Yaks. This appears to have been fairly one-sided, since the overall victory of the Tigers in 1946 was heralded as their first triumph for many years. In summer 1951, the T.Y. system was reintroduced as a termly competition[6] (presumably meaning in the form of house points, as currently obtains), and it is probably from this time that tokens or tallies were first issued, each bearing the legend St John's Competition and the initials T Y. The surviving specimens are thin

5 Prefect's Log, January 1942ff.

6 The Beaumont Review, vol. XXIII, no. 175 (July 1951), 238. A confusing statement, even if it had been a yearly competition before that, since the School rolls bear the 'Competition' heading from summer 1947. The Yaks won at Christmas 1950 with a score of 6199 to the Tigers' 5877, after which official records of such achievements are scanty.

paper slips, roughly the size of a banknote, printed in blue or grey; a single example in green on slightly heavier paper may be a model for other issues or a sole remnant of the change of colour for the Yaks. Score cards arrived later. The division of marks into meritorious subdivisions of COMITAS[7] is a twenty-first century scheme; early cards merely recorded positive or negative.

By June 1944, the Blitz was long passed, and matters were relatively quiescent, as epitomised by the closing paragraph from the Sports Day programme that year, which gave thanks for general good health, and recorded the antics of the school's Scottish terrier. Into this cheerfully optimistic summer atmosphere came Christopher Roberts, aged seven and three-quarters. Having entered at an awkward point in the academic year, he then spent four terms in Preparatory (his classroom being that which is now the School Office at the top of the main stairs next to the senior dormitory), before moving up to Elements I in September 1945.

We followed the progress of battles through the newspapers which were laid out on the billiard table. I remember we had a half-holiday on the day Rome was surrendered without fighting [and] we processed with the Great Litanies all around the school. The sounds of war were familiar to us all, the drone of fleets of bombers leaving their vapour trails across the sky on their way to Germany, the occasional [nocturnal] rumble of a German bomber overhead, the rumble of anti-aircraft fire from the guns in Windsor Great Park, but most of all the night-time explosion of the V1 that hit The Bells of Ouseley. We Preparatory boarders were sleeping under the main staircase at that time and I am sure we heard the swish of the bomb as it glided down parallel with the slope of Priest Hill. The school walked down the next day to see the damage.[8]

Tuesday 9th [April 1945]. Victory day.
A.M. free, with Treasure Hunt on drive. P.M. Churchill's announcement heard by boys in rec room. This was followed by Penny Sports, followed by tuck at 5.30. Benediction at 6.00 Te Deum in English and Domine salvam fac, with Faith of our Fathers. Solemn benediction. Supper or rather High Tea (very very good) at 6.30. Fair organised by Scouts in playground. 9.00 King's Speech – all out 9.45 Bonfire. 10.30 cocoa in playroom served by Fr Ferguson. 11.00 Bed.[9]

Several windows at Beaumont College (including the rose window in the chapel) were blown in by the memorable explosion from the bomb that destroyed The Bells, but St John's itself was almost unscathed by both international conflicts, sustaining little damage to the fabric. Indeed, when claims were made for repairs, the representative of the War Damage Commission was unable to agree to them, since

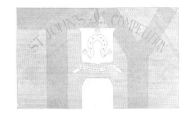

Early TYs.

7 Conscientious, Organised, Manners, Impressive, Truthful, Attentive, Selfless.

8 Roberts, Christopher. Email to author, 7 January 2015

9 Prefect's Log, January 1942ff, ibid.

A.M.D.G.                    TOY CLUB.

Lino Club was far too expensive a club for war time. It is therefore making these changes: You pay 1/- to join, and never pay another halfpenny for anything. Lino and paper will be free: tools will be "Pool" tools. Plasticine has been bought and if you want to make plasticine models, you just take some and return it when it is done, to its proper box. Matchboxes and corks, acorns and cedar cones, clay and wood will all be got in order that Toys may be made of them. The Boy Scouts will be the managers of the club when they can help. Work is in Elements on half holidays at tea-time. Rowdy ways not allowed. The Lino Club is now the Toy Model Club. Those who don't want their tools to be "Pooled", remove them at once.

he had obtained information that the majority of the defects were pre-war. Only some minor cracks in the dormitory ceilings bore testament to the troubled years.

The two most impressive items in a crowded year have been the flying bombs and V-Day. Both went off with a bang. Our overworked Te Deum at Benediction on V-Day had to express our gratitude for six years of Divine protection, for we did not lose even a pane of glass.[10] There was little in our V-Day celebrations to suggest a lasting peace. The hunt for Mars Bars on Victory morning brought temporary relief ... but it was with the five-course dinner that Victory arrived. Tinned peaches and other reserves, saved for a possible German invasion, were hastily thrown in to stabilize our front. There were many bulges and bottlenecks.[11]

The July 1945 issue of *The Beaumont Review* lists those serving in the Forces, among whom is SPENCE, E.H.D., Sqr-Ldr, RAF, VR — so the boy who wrote the postcards to his mother in 1910 lived through all the tumultuous times.

10 At this point, a similar account published in the Sports Day programme for 23 June 1945 remarks: Father Sharkey and Father Ferguson alone remember the 700lb bomb which fell just beyond the cricket field on 4th October 1940, and the other bombs on Priests' [sic] Hill. They can challenge the verdict of Elements Two that the doodle bug which flew low over us last summer was "the best bit of the whole war".

11 *The Beaumont Review*, vol. XXII, no. 163 (July 1945), 108. The Mars factory at Slough opened in 1932 and provided regular treats to the boys, as well as hosting the occasional visit.

12 In fact, no solar eclipse occurred during these years that would have been visible from the UK; so, as this activity definitely involved projecting an image of the sun via a telescope, it was most probably an experiment to view sunspots.

The autumn term activities included expeditions on the Beeches to collect blackberries, and into Beaumont woods for rosehips. The former were made into jam or apple and blackberry puddings, the latter into rosehip syrup (for matron) by the nuns. Football was the great winter game plus British Bulldogs and Release-O in the woods.

[My time in] Elements II (September 1946 to July 1947), was a wonderful year with Mr. Northover. Apart from basic studies he gave us such a [superb] grounding in natural history. We were learning *Hiawatha*, so we built a model of his lakeside village and animals. Big old sweet jars were filled with ants' nests so we could see how their colonies worked, and in summer we fed and kept caterpillars, watching them pupate. It may have been that summer that Fr. Ferguson set up his telescope on the cricket pitch so that we could all see a partial eclipse.[12] That winter [1947] of course was truly memorable. I think it started snowing about 10th January, real heavy snow like few of us had seen before. The frosts were fearsome, day and night. Today we would have been sent home: 'Sorry, School closed'. Not possible then as all transport was stuck, not to mention petrol rationing. The miners were on strike, it snowed, the railways were jammed, it snowed, roads were closed, even I think Priest Hill for a time. All the while it snowed and froze. All lessons were taken wearing overcoats and gloves as there was little fuel for heating. Figures I and II went skating on the Cow Pond in Windsor Great Park. Tobogganing was the great outdoor game. The field between the playground and Priest Hill ran down from the Beeches to the school farm; it was a vast gutter of deep snow and the ideal toboggan run. After snowball fights between Tigers and Yaks, it was not long before the hillside was a sheet of packed frozen snow. Toboggans of all sorts appeared: anything that was flat and could be laid on or sat on. There were no plastic sheets or bin liners then. The best one-man sledge was a tin tray from the Infirmary: they went like a rocket but were a bit unstable. However ... one afternoon the big sledge, a sheet of tin with several boys on board, was hurtling down the hill. Unfortunately Christopher Wilkinson did not hear it coming — sixty boys out on the snow make quite a noise — and he was hit. Pandemonium followed as the poor chap was rushed to the infirmary and Dr. Cunningham summoned; he may have gone to Windsor Hospital. When he came back, he had a long cut down his thigh and a mass of stitches [which] probably stayed with him well into later life. That ended multi-boyed toboggans, but individual tobogganing and snowballing continued until finally the snow melted. The Thames had terrific floods and even the ferry at the Bells of Ouseley had to stop. Needless to say the summer that followed was fantastic and by the next term Chris was the proud owner of a hero's scar.

[The chapel] organ was the pride of Tommy Clayton our most marvellous music master. It stood in the organ loft and was hand pumped, usually by two members of the First XV who could not sing. For normal Benediction or High Mass it was fairly smooth going, but for those pumping on special occasions with visitors to impress in the pew below or [when the organist] felt in the best of moods, a Bach Toccata and Fugue or a 'Pomp & Circumstance' would produce a sweat on the best of men. That wretched little ivory float that measured the air available could go down amazingly quickly. Mind you, the pumpers did get their reward on St Cecilia's feast when they joined the choir supper.

I left SJB in Summer 1949. I think the extra term in 1944 made [my tenure at the school] one of the longest.[13]

In the past years, Almighty God has showered favours on St. John's. Immunity from raids is a cause for gratitude. Further, in the past two years we have been bursting with boys who themselves have been bursting with good health. There has been no serious illness and only one epidemic in two years. Our new Matron, whom we warmly welcome, would be in for an easy time were it not for coupons and clothes. These are bursting, like their owners, and Matron has her job cut out keeping us clean. Also, she has "J" to look after, a very small Scotch terrier who will soon be old enough to join Preparatory. He was given fifty lines yesterday for eating two buttons, which in war-time are urgently needed at the front.

*Above:* Excerpt from Sports Day programme, 1944.

*Opposite:* Toy Club in wartime: Prefect's Log, 1942.

13 Roberts, Christopher. Email to author, ibid.

Detail of entrance hall ceiling over fireplace.

*Opposite:* Underside of keystone in entrance porch.

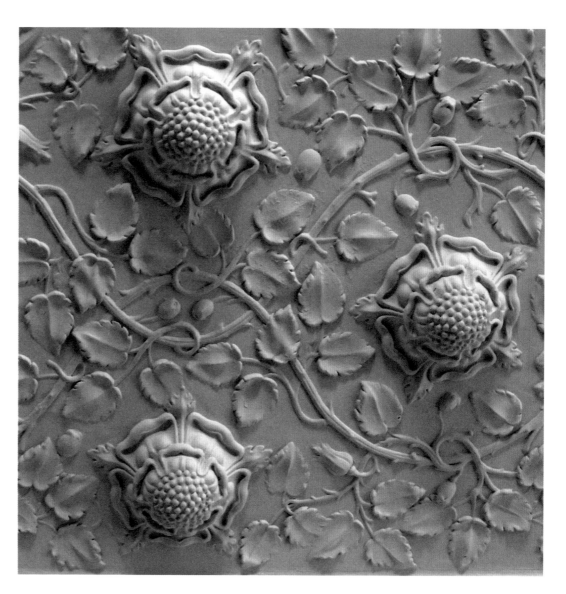

# 7. New Elizabethans

As the 1950s dawned, the roll of St John's remained at some seventy boys. Such a number would be practically unviable today, but there was then little room or desire for growth. A few day boys supplemented the sixty boarders, who were the heart of the School. Beaumont College was flourishing, and evidence suggests that the core clientele of St John's wished matters to continue as they had always done; but the world had, in fact, changed irrevocably. Over the remaining years of the century, St John's expanded, although the College closed in 1967 and the governors of Stonyhurst took over responsibility for its younger brother. While developments in communication and transport no doubt helped it retain its international appeal, St John's also greatly increased its development plans, broadened its demographic intake, and developed its syllabus, provisions and outlook beyond recognition. Members of the cast of *Alice* from 1938 would have been familiar with the Gryphon's cynical maxim, 'That's the reason they're called lessons because they lessen from day to day.' Readers may like to test the truth of his opinion by attempting the post-war paper shown here. Jesuit tenets and the Roman Catholic faith remained at the heart of the school, but the facilities and possibilities available to the pupils at its centenary would have seemed astounding to those who, at its opening in the tranquil rural lanes of Victorian Old Windsor, were still marvelling at the miracle of electric light.

The centenary celebrations of Beaumont College in 1961 attracted the attention of the national press, including a four-page photographic spread in *The Sphere*,[1] in which it was mentioned that the roll at St John's was almost ninety boys. In order to ease the cramped conditions that year, an extension over the Lady Gallery was completed and divided into two rooms: one for Art, the other a dark room for the Photo Club. As a single space, this is now the boarders' Den.

> By Monday 21st January [1963], the Thames at Old Windsor was frozen over as far as the eye could see in both directions, except for a passage cut in the ice for the ferry boat. Two days later, even this passage had disappeared. This state of affairs provided, at least, something for the records as all the boys were able to walk upon the Thames.[2]

*Opposite:* Eager frequenters of the School Shop, possibly situated in what is now the small meeting room opposite the Refectory. Undated.

*Below*: Comics in the Playroom, undated.

1 *The Sphere,* vol. CCXLV, no. 3180 (May 13, 1961), 247. The issue also includes an illustrated report on H.M. Queen Elizabeth's state visit to Rome that year, including an audience with Pope John XXIII.

2 *The Beaumont Review*, vol. XXIX, no. 206 (June 1963), 394

Left: St John's, 1950.
Back row: M. Gillivan, A. Stevens, R. Bellamy, R. Waller, S. de la Bedoyere, A. d'Ombrain, J. Tristram, A. Synnott, R. Dawney, N. Warren, G. Dines, P. Johansen.
4th row: D. McCurry, P. Walker, J. Cuddigan, H. Stevens, J. Becvar, P. Hilterman, P. Flaherty, C. Johnson, D. Henry, N. Aldington, F. Staples, R. Rutherford, S. Oliver, A. Hinds, R. Roddy, G. Hinds.
3rd row: B McNamee, A Morrogh, M. Stickney, S. O'Sullivan, A. Hussey, A. Harty, N. Quine, K. O'Sullivan, D. Pendry, J. Patrizzy, J. Pendry, D. de Weck, P. Bicknell, A. Miles, J. de Trafford, M. Walsh, J. Kenny, J. Lightfoot.

2nd row: J. Dias, M. Shields, D. Bulfield, I. Sinclair, J. Hanrahan, B. Murray, A. Wyatt, R. Murphy, A. Thompson, A. Rait, S. Jones, D. Lightfoot, J. McAleer, J. Compertz, J. Rossage, J. Iverson.
Front row: J. Smallman, P. Pritchard, S. Stevens, N. Walter, M. Bulfield, D. Hamilton, W. Bovell-Jones, M. Bingham, M. Barr, A. Halsey de Kerdrel, P. Doyle, A. Stickney, M. Wigan, P. Agnew, P. Hamilton.

Above: 1st XV Rugby, 1951–1952.
Back row: A. Bellamy, S. Oliver, S. O'Sullivan, C. Lake, M. Wood, A Ruane.
Second row: C. Johnson, S. McCurry, J. Becvar (capt.), H. Stevens, P. Flaherty.
Front row: A. Stickney, M. Bulfield, N. Warren, A. Stevens.

**June 16th, 1952.**  **No. 5.**

## COMMON EXAMINATION FOR
## ENTRANCE TO PUBLIC SCHOOLS.

---

### GEOMETRY.

[*60 minutes.*]

**All boys must do as much of A as they can before going on to B. In Question I no description of the construction used need be written but the figure must show clearly the method of construction.**

### A.

I. Draw a triangle ABC in which $\angle$ ABC = 43°, AB = 2·7in., and BC = 3·2in. Measure $\angle$ ACB.

Using the same figure, construct the line bisecting $\angle$ BAC without using a protractor. If this line meets BC at X, measure BX.

II. In Fig. 1, PQ is parallel to RS, RMQ is a straight line and RM = RN. If $\angle$ PQR = 42°, calculate $\angle$ QMN, giving reasons fully.

III. In Fig. 2, $\triangle$ ABC and $\triangle$ QMF are congruent scalene triangles. If it is known that $\angle$ ABC = $\angle$ QMF, which side in $\triangle$ ABC must be equal to which side in $\triangle$ QMF and why? If also $\angle$ BAC = $\angle$ MQF, which side in $\triangle$ QMF is equal to BC and why?

IV. A, B are two points 6 cm. apart. What is the locus of a variable point which is 3·2 cm. from A? What is the locus of a variable point which is 2·8 cm. from B? Draw an accurate figure in addition to giving your answers shortly in words.

### B.

**N.B.—Begin Part B on a new sheet.**

V. In fig. 3, the triangles ABL and ACK are equilateral triangles. Prove that the triangles LAC, BAK are congruent.

VI. In fig. 4, AD is parallel to KBC, $\angle$ AKB = 90°, AK = 4 cm., BC = 6 cm., AD = 10 cm., AC = 8 cm. Calculate :—

    (i) the area of the triangle ABC ;

    (ii) the area of the trapezium ABCD ;

    (iii) the length of the perpendicular from B to AC.

[P. T. O.

---

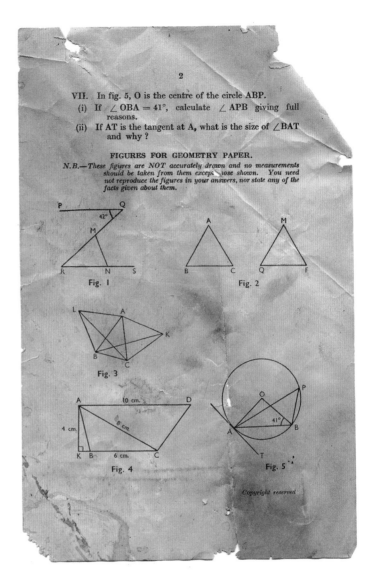

2

VII. In fig. 5, O is the centre of the circle ABP.

  (i) If $\angle$ OBA = 41°, calculate $\angle$ APB giving full reasons.

  (ii) If AT is the tangent at A, what is the size of $\angle$ BAT and why ?

### FIGURES FOR GEOMETRY PAPER.

*N.B.—These figures are NOT accurately drawn and no measurements should be taken from them except those shown. You need not reproduce the figures in your answers, nor state any of the facts given about them.*

---

Common Entrance Geometry paper, 16 June 1952.

*Opposite, clockwise from top left (all undated):* Weighty matters; Practical recreation; Drama reading or choral speaking in the Playroom; Young artists; The latest instalment.

It may be reflected here how extra-curricular activities, particularly the games programme, have changed over the years. St John's has always been known for its rugby, and this dedication continues, but swimming has a very firm place, while a myriad of other activities take place regularly. In the early post-war years, St John's was known particularly for its boxing prowess. The sport had been relished since at least 1904, and there were soon Boxing Carnivals every Shrovetide. However, its zenith was in 1948, when the team won six out of nine matches against other schools, while the Scout Troop competed in a district competition, and won every fight they entered: which was practically everything available to them.[3] Boxing was not taught in state schools after 1962, although independent schools continued to promote it.

St John's did not seek the limelight, being content to carry on its mission through the years in its own quiet yet individual manner. Its early clientele and distinguished alumni must have secured a sense of worth, and rendered exhibitionism and evangelism unnecessary. However, the occasional incognito appearance of the School itself has gained it a small place in media footnotes. In May 1960, the new outdoor swimming pool (opened four years earlier after decades in the planning), was used for several shots in *A French Mistress*, a riotous farce in the style of the Ealing comedies, with a veteran cast including James Robertson Justice and Irene Handl.[4] 'The pool had to be heated for the occasion, and the arrival and positioning of the magnificent steam engine which did the job — and

*Opposite:* Daring dive, *c.*1965.

*Below:* Boxing, *c.*1960.

3 *The Beaumont Review*, vol. XXII, no. 169 (July 1948), 182

4 Charter Film Productions, 1961 (b&w). Roy Boulting *producer*, Sonny Hale *writer*, Mutz Greenbaum *cinematography*, John Addison *music*.

Photocard, *c.*1914.

*Opposite:* A murder has been arranged: Berchmans' Library, *c.*1965.

43. Gymnasium, St John's, Beaumont College.

very satisfactorily too — was an event in itself. One excellent result was that the boys were able to swim on the Saturday afternoon as the water was so warm!'[5] In 1987, the front façade of St John's was transformed into the Oxford Foreign Examinations Syndicate for 'The Silent World of Nicholas Quinn', the second episode of the iconic TV series *Inspector Morse*.[6] Views of the newly-built indoor pool were carefully avoided, while camera trickery placed the school a couple of miles or so from the trees of central Oxford. Among the interiors, the main gallery, the Entrance Hall, and a rejuvenated Berchmans' Library where the murder took place (the producer particularly relished the graceful window lights) are easily identifiable.

Fr Bernard Walker became headmaster in 1978, and it was under his leadership that the Emus at last appeared within the TYE system, their emergence doubtless prompted by the increase in pupil numbers. It is not yet clear exactly why this creature was chosen above such possibilities as Eagles or Egrets, or indeed, Elephants. One theory links the bird to fraternal Australian establishments, such as St Aloysius' College in Sydney or St Ignatius' College in Adelaide, but it seems most probable that the overall choice was guided by the addition of a creature whose initial would not alter the established pronunciation of TY. The Emus first appeared on the Inter-Animal Relay Race trophy in 1988, although there is a gap in the dates between 1970 and 1986, both of which were Tiger victories.

5 *The Beaumont Review*, vol. XXIX, no. 198 (October 1960), 20

6 Carlton Television, 1987. Colin Dexter *writer*, Kenny McBain *producer*, Barrington Pheloung *music*, starring John Thaw, Kevin Whateley, and Michael Gough. It is a curious coincidence, although no more than that, to find a Nicholas Quine in the photo from summer 1950 (above).

Sports Days. *Clockwise from top left:*
Archery display, *c.*1975.

Brian O'Flynn at scoreboard, 1992.

Tug of war on front field, with Fr Budworth, 1965.

*Opposite*: Gym, undated.

Distinguished guests of varying status who have occasionally graced the School are headed by H.M. Queen Elizabeth II, who visited Beaumont College in 1961 to mark its centenary (at which time she also greeted the St John's boys), and made a return visit to Old Windsor in October 2009 to open the Dermot Gogarty Sports Centre. Other personalities have included Anneka Rice in May 1989 (an off-shoot from the recently launched BBC television programme *Challenge Anneka*, in aid of Comic Relief), Sir Cliff Richard, who performed with the Chapel Choir and other school musicians for a charity concert in 2012 — sadly for some, our close neighbour Sir Elton John has never crossed the intervening fields — and, perhaps most astonishingly, Mother Teresa of Calcutta, who paid what was evidently an extraordinary visit in 1993. Following a parental contact through one of her charities, she spent just a short half-hour outside the School with the boys, a breathless meeting sandwiched between a previous engagement and a flight from Heathrow.

Of all the luminaries who have shaped St John's, the name of Dermot Gogarty must surely rank among the highest. An immensely charismatic and visionary leader who galvanised colleagues and pupils alike, he was only 29 when he succeeded the first lay Headmaster, Brian Duffy, in 1987. Born in South Africa, Gogarty obtained a first-class degree in history at the University of Cape

*Opposite and above:* Royal visit, 1961. Note the Imperatores' medals.

*Above:* Mother Teresa, 1993.

H.M. The Queen opens the
Dermot Gogarty Sports Centre,
2009.

Town, moving to the UK in response to the regime of apartheid. Under his headmastership, the School's reputation rose to stellar heights, and a substantial programme of building and expansion created a pre-prep department (the Nicholas Owen Block), a new library, the STAC (Science, Technology and Art Centre), and a Music School, with modest theatre adjacent, named after Fr David Hoy. Gogarty's tragically early death in a car crash in 2005 at the age of 47 was an unprecedented blow to the foundation, and the emotional shockwaves have still not quite subsided. A Trust established in his memory supports the work of Old Boys wishing to engage in community activities among the less fortunate, often in developing countries. His determination to improve the sporting facilities at St John's was achieved posthumously through the Centre named after him.

Thanks in no small measure to these ventures, St John's in its one hundred and twenty-fifth year remained strong in many areas, but most notably in its impressive string of scholarships in music, art and sport. The last-named has produced some extraordinary achievements, such as a relay swim of the English Channel by four boys and two adults. The arts, one of the most important facets of a civilised society, are in a very real sense core subjects, affecting nearly everyone's lives daily, either passively or though the deep appreciation of universal languages that go beyond words. They expose their practitioners and listeners to the numinous. In addition to nurturing the gifted and talented, the Music and Art Schools are focussed on awakening and sustaining the diverse interests, passions and skills of all the boys to their full potential. It is now hard to imagine Art being taught in the boarders' Den, or music being created in what is now the tiny meeting room opposite the Playroom, which, in St John's earliest days, was the sole physical provision for non-sacred music. The Chapel Choir continues to prosper at the heart of the School, but pictorial evidence from early days is rare, since the boys were usually out of sight in the organ gallery. Composition now flourishes in all styles, recitals are given by distinguished soloists and ensembles, and there is a healthy environment of cross-disciplinary studies, which has resulted in some exciting collaborations, ranging from stage design to the very latest developments in international digital media.

*Top: Dermot St John Gogarty* by Ian McKillop. Oil on canvas, 2006.

*Above:* Dermot St John Gogarty. Headmaster 1987–2005.

St John's has no intention of disappearing into the sunset. Rather, it will continue to open doors, with the intention that its achievements in the twenty-first century will be as memorable and enthralling as those of the past.

*All That Jazz* by Cody Mok,
artist and pianist. Acrylic on
canvas, 2013.

*Movement in Music* by
Keisuke Sano, violinist and
artist. Acrylic on canvas, 2013.

*Clockwise from top left:*
Treble soloists and composers with ensemble EXAUDI in chapel, 2014. *Front row, left to right:* Crispin Kerr-Dineen, Luke Gifford, Linus Lampe, Alex Kazin, Eric Li, Oscar Eddis, Astemir Azhakhov.

Head Chorister's medal, 2015.

Chapel Choristers at Christmas, 2014. Wills Bayldon-Pritchard, Leonardo Haitzmann, Daniel Bennett.

*Opposite, clockwise from top left:*
Jack Spink *electric guitar.*

Trumpeter, undated.

Flutes and clarinets, undated.

Chapel Choir, Sports Day, 1965.

String Quartet, 2013:
Ben Steiner *cello,* Alvin Chan *violin II,* Ethan Shum *viola,* Keisuke Sano *violin I.*

*Opposite:* Decoration on right of main façade.

Window, front façade.

The symbols of St John Berchmans by the east window of the chapel: rosary, cross, and the Rule Book of the Society of Jesus, being the three objects he asked to be brought to him on his death-bed. St John was widely regarded as a saint in his own lifetime, and evidence for his canonisation was being collected within a year of his death.

# Appendix

*Carmen Beaumontanum* and the legacy of Fr John Driscoll

The loyal song of Beaumont College was a typical product of the late Victorian period, a time when almost every educational establishment, however modest, boasted an anthem extolling its nobility and merits, replete with dedications, pledges, four-square phrases and hearty exhortations that the foundation should flourish. *Carmen Beaumontanum* was written in 1885 by Fr George Kingdon SJ (Prefect of Studies at the College from 1879 to 1887), and set to music at the same time by Samuel Smith, music master from 1862 to 1903. The song remained in constant use for the majority of the College's life until its closure in 1967, and has retained a loyal following among Old Boys. It was therefore natural that St John's on its opening should adopt what was then almost a brand-new piece, although the new millennium found it largely fallen into disuse. In 2012, the then Assistant Director of Music, Dr Deborah Mollison, composed a new song with words by Pauline Southcombe that incorporated the Jesuit motto *Ad majorem Dei gloriam*. Its striding sequential tune was an immediate success and, at the time of writing, it looks set to have as long a life as its predecessor.

When sacred music was required, the College and St John's were both indebted to Fr John Driscoll, SJ, a name now little-known. An outstanding preacher but also an eminent authority on voice production and choir training, particularly of boys' voices, his work was lauded by such luminaries as Stanford, Vaughan Williams, Gervase Elwes and Ernest Newman. Driscoll was appointed director of the choir at the Sacred Heart Church, Wimbledon in 1904, a position he retained until his death in 1940. From 1928 he combined this post with a similar appointment at the superb Jesuit Church of the Immaculate Conception, Farm Street, Mayfair, always displaying utter dedication and musicianship in his duties.[1] Through much of the early years of the twentieth century, Driscoll was at work on his *Cantionale*, a collection of sacred music tailored initially to the requirements of Wimbledon, then Stonyhurst and Beaumont, with a posthumous edition for Harlaxton. A hymnal and anthem-collection combined, St John's inherited the volume and its traditions as a matter of course. The contents of the *Cantionale* were compiled from numerous sources, making it suitable for almost any and every liturgical necessity, while its status 'in usum nostrorum' permitted the official inclusion of many tunes that would otherwise be copyright. Driscoll's preface explained his rationale.

1 One of his successors was the distinguished organist and teacher Nicholas Danby, an old boy of St John's. On Palm Sunday 1945, when in Elements II, Danby was the winner in the Second Set for the Elocution Prize, reciting *You are Old, Father William* with 'great confidence and charm': see *The Beaumont Review*, vol. XXII, no. 163 (July 1945), 108. In the later pantomime of *Robinson Crusoe* he took the role of the Demon King 'with the precise diction of a Shakespearian actor': see *The Beaumont Review*, vol. XXIII, no. 165 (April 1946), 151.

# Carmen Beaumontanum

**With spirit**

Con - ci - na - mus gna - vi - ter, Om - nes Beau - mon - ta - ni, Vo - cem de - mus sua - vi - ter,

No - vi,___ Ve - te - ra - ni; Et si___ mox pug - na - vi - mus, Jam con - da - mus eu - ses,

CHORUS

Seu Ro - ma - ni fu - i - mus, Seu Car - tha - gi - nen - ses. Nun - quam sit per sae - cu - la

*rall.*

De - cus___ is - tud___ va - num, Vi - vat si - ne ma - cu - la___ No - men Beau - mon - ta - num.

Vi - vat___

Fr John Driscoll, SJ.

In choosing these tunes for college use an effort has been made to find a *via media* between the noisy fireworks and cloying chromaticisms of the Victorians on the one hand and on the other the glacial archaism and flaccid placidity affected by many today as the hall-mark of good taste. Youth is not concerned with fashions in music. All it wants is a tune that will grip and stir the devotional pulse ... Consequently, in this collection, sturdy, broad virile tunes, when available have been requisitioned ... No tune of whatever school or date or nationality, has been rejected if found worthy as music and suitable for the purpose of this work ... [2]

In other words, this was by no means a standard anthology, even for the comparatively limited resources for which it was assembled. Everything was fair game, including those works on which the ink was barely dry; and armed with such strength of purpose, Driscoll went a-plundering. The Beaumont edition eventually saw publication in 1940, a few months before the death of its compiler on 6 December that year. It is a fascinating read, particularly for students of hymnology, and left an indelible mark on the music of St John's. The bombastic setting of the *Pater Noster* by the Swiss composer Abraham Louis Niedermeyer (1802–1861)[3] is still sung there, and at Stonyhurst, while the gentler traditional carol *Come to the manger* was an indispensable ingredient of Christmas celebrations at Beaumont and St John's for some years (the College made a private recording of it in 1962). However, while Driscoll's social objectives were no doubt admirable, it is clear that he was also not a whit concerned about fashions in music. Only the purpose and the outcome mattered. As a result, the publication is a curious example of zeal outpacing integrity, with many works having new texts in Latin or English imposed on them; and while the composers chosen are usually acknowledged with some deference, their original titles are rarely indicated. Unlike a writer seeking suitable tunes for his verses[4], Driscoll's opposite approach was to begin with a rousing tune, and then assign a text to it. This piracy frequently resulted in 'one song to the tune of another' that quickly became a reliable source of unintentional hilarity for the cognoscenti; indeed, the majority of his changeling compositions, many reproduced in the *Cantionale*, still appear decidedly curious today. What, one wonders, was the musical or theological reasoning in seizing the two immortal settings of *In the bleak midwinter* by Holst and Darke, but trading Rossetti's lines for a Marian invocation by F W Faber? Brahms' lullaby reawoken as a carol, *Though the stable be cold*, and Mendelssohn's familiar tune to *Hark! the herald-angels sing* transposed to a different season as *By the first bright Easter day* are further examples of quirky liaisons. Even *Londonderry Air* — which, as Driscoll acknowledges, is considered by the Jesuit musicologist Dr Gratton Flood to be of religious origin — became a similar Christmas offering, *As long ago, men o'er*

2 Driscoll, John (ed.). Preface to *Beaumont Cantionale: hymns Latin and English*. S.l., s.n. (1940).

3 A friend of Rossini, the college bearing his name was the alma mater of Fauré and Messager.

4 An early example is *Christmas Carols or Sacred Songs suited to The Festival of Our Lord's Nativity with Appropriate Music* (an obscure and anonymous collection published in 1833 in connection with the SPCK) that harnesses various melodies, including examples by Handel, Arne and Haydn, to seasonal texts. Among the pages are Christmas verses attached to a close variant of the Easter carol from *Lyra Davidica* (1708), now generally sung as *Jesus Christ is ris'n today*; and a Marian eulogy allied to a major-key harmonisation of *God rest ye merry, gentlemen*. The author is grateful to Stephen Banfield for drawing his attention to this volume.

*their flocks were keeping.* If Driscoll considered an existing text unsuitable for his purposes, he was quick to replace it with his own verses, regardless of whether they fitted especially well or not. A particularly ironic example is Vaughan Williams' fine *Withers' Rocking Hymn*, which became *My Son, teach me what words to use* (those of George Withers evidently being found wanting). Other extraordinary borrowings from Vaughan Williams are his cheerful hymn tune *Sine nomine* ('For all the Saints') converted to a solemn prayer for souls in purgatory; and an *Alma coelestium* set to *Down Ampney* ('Come down, O love divine') — which, being far too brief for the task, segues immediately at the refrain of the new text into Martin Shaw's *Little Cornard* (indissolubly wedded to 'Hills of the North, rejoice') without the slightest attempt being made to disguise the conjunction. Many other familiar melodies sound disquietingly, not to say jarringly, eccentric when paired with unrelated Latin hymns: the prime instance is perhaps Holst's great tune from 'Jupiter' pressed into service as a *Venite concinemus.* However, one example in the *Cantionale* where a new text might be thought to have improved the original is Peter Warlock's *The Five Lesser Joys of Mary*, published barely four years before. Driscoll noted of the composer: 'Well known for his highly artistic songs. His promising career was cut short by premature death'. The original weak text by Laurence Kelleher (which is fey and does not scan properly) was then rejected — probably for theological reasons[5] — and substituted with Driscoll's own translation of words from the Greek of St John Damascene, which begins:

> In Bethlehem town ere the break of the dawn
> The Lord, as he willed, in a stable was born.
> To Thee Whose bright throne spans the arches of Heav'n
> A manger to lie in 'mid oxen was giv'n.

Driscoll hated ostentation in all forms, working as far as possible out of the public eye, yet his undoubted achievements could never quite stifle his nagging doubts that his life's calling had hindered the full development of his religious and spiritual studies.[6] It would therefore do him a disservice to be too hard on him or to make the *Cantionale*, compiled for a specific purpose, his memorial. Rather, it is his towering achievements in the field of choral music that ought to be celebrated. In this art form, along with his contemporary Sir Richard Terry at Westminster Cathedral whose carol arrangements and liturgical music were regularly heard at St John's, he raised the Catholic liturgy to great heights, and blazed the trail for such pupils and successors as George Malcolm. His published legacy may strike one as curious and questionable, but his dedication and devotion cannot be doubted. He deserves to be remembered.

5 One suspects that Driscoll would have had particular doubts about the fourth and fifth Joys in Kelleher's enumeration. Neither is exactly Lesser: the finding of Jesus in the Temple, and the Crucifixion are, respectively, the fifth Joyful and fifth Sorrowful Mysteries of the Rosary.

6 See also Lillie, H W R, *Father John Driscoll SJ: a memoir.* London: Manresa Press (n.d.).

# Acknowledgments

I wish to thank the Headmaster of St John's, Mr Giles Delaney, and the Bursar, Mr Tim Blad, who commissioned this volume, and granted me unrestricted access to the school archives; and for the great support of Anna Edwards at the Archivum Britannicum Societatis Iesu. While the historical images are largely from these two institutions, the majority of the colour photography has been especially contributed by Dominic James. The finished article is testament to the superb professionalism of Richard and Sam Adams; it was an enormous pleasure working with them again.

My research was aided by the staff of English Heritage, the Imperial War Museum, and British Library Newspapers, Colindale; while the archivists of the Victoria and Albert Museum provided invaluable insight in allowing me to view J.F. Bentley's extremely fragile working papers and designs. Special gratitude is due to Christopher Roberts for sharing his vivid experiences of St John's in the 1940s: his emailed recollections are quoted with minimal and silent editing. I am also indebted to Fr Adrian Porter SJ for his knowledge and clarification of many matters.

For approval to include photographs of themselves or their work, I am happy to acknowledge the following: Astemir Azhakhov, Wills Bayldon-Pritchard, Daniel Bennett, Joe Bowman, Alvin Chan, Oscar Eddis, Luke Gifford, Leonardo Haitzmann, Hugo Huggins, Alex Kazin, Crispin Kerr-Dineen, Linus Lampe, Eric Li, Ian McKillop, Cody Mok, Keisuke Sano, Ethan Shum, Jack Spink, Ben Steiner, and the vocal ensemble EXAUDI.

The following have also given of their time, and assisted in diverse ways: Colin Ballantyne, Paola Bright, Geraldine Calder, Ted Coyle, Juliette Hall, Lukas and Leonardo Haitzmann, Derek Halstead, Daniela Harwood, Maria Martin, Katherine Masterson, Dr Deborah Mollison, Martina Prentis, Sarah Taylor, and Mark Walker. To them I am most grateful; to any others I may have inadvertently omitted, I offer my belated thanks and apologies.

*First Impressions* by Ian McKillop. Oil on plywood, 2002.

*Study of Magritte* by Hugo Huggins. Acrylic on canvas, 2014.

# About the author

Andrew Plant has been Director of Music at St John's Beaumont since 2011, having previously taught at Uppingham, and St George's School, Windsor Castle. He was awarded his doctorate from the University of Birmingham, where he was a visiting lecturer, and spent almost a decade as a musicologist on the staff of The Britten–Pears Foundation. As a piano accompanist, he regularly partners some of the world's finest singers throughout the UK and abroad, with recent concerts in France, Slovenia and Russia.